WHAT IS IN A NAME?

The History of Alberta Federal Riding Names

E.G. Mardon & A. A. Mardon
Edited by Claire MacMaster

A Golden Meteorite Press Book.

© 2012 copyright by Ernest Mardon, and Austin Mardon,

Printed in Canada by Golden Meteorite Press.

No part of this publication may be reproduced, stored in a retrieval system or transmitted, in any form or by any means, without prior written consent of the publisher or a licence from The Canadian Copyright Licensing Agency (Access Copyright). For an Access Copyright licence, visit www.accesscopyright.ca or call toll free to 1-800-893-5777.

Cover design and typeset by Bianca Ho
Edited by Claire MacMaster

Published by Golden Meteorite Press.
126 Kingsway Garden
Post Office Box 34181,
Edmonton, Alberta, CANADA.
T5G 3G4
Telephone: 1-(780)-378-0063
Email: aamardon@yahoo.ca
Web site: www.austinmardon.org

Library and Archives Canada Cataloguing in Publication

Mardon, Ernest G., 1928-
    What is in a name? : the history of Alberta federal riding names / E.G. Mardon & A.A. Mardon.

ISBN 978-1-897472-58-3

    1. Election districts--Alberta--History. 2. Canada. Parliament--Election districts. 3. Names, Geographical--Alberta. 4. Alberta--History, Local. 5. Legislators--Canada--Biography. I. Mardon, Austin A. (Austin Albert) II. Title.

FC3656.M37 2012   971.23   C2012-904772-4

*Dedicated to
Teresa Mardon*

WHAT IS IN A NAME?

The History of Alberta Federal Riding Names

*Though our sins may be scarlet,
we hope our book is read.*

Contents

Preface..11
Chapter One: Place Names..12
        The History of Place Names................18
        I. Names Derived from Nature............20
        II. Aboriginal Names.......................22
        III. Fur and Whiskey Traders................24
        IV. The Coming of Law and Order........26
        V. Surveyors and the Coming
           of the Iron Horse............................27
        Names of Alberta............................33
Chapter Two: Biographies..52
Members of the House of Commons Elected
        From Alberta Constituencies...............54
        Biographies of Senators
        From Alberta...................................101
        Chronological List of Alberta
        Chief Justices...................................124
        Alberta Federal Ridings With the
        Names of Members of Parliament
        With Their Party Affiliations...............128
        Alphabetical List of Senators
        From Alberta...................................147
Maps and Charts...150
List of Alberta Ridings..155
Authors' Works...162

Preface

Names, especially place names are a fascinating study. Their very variety prompts one to ask from whence they came. The was certainly true of Federal Ridings in 1887 when the District of Alberta, N.W.T., was granted the right to send on elected member to the House of Commons and it is still true today. The names of ridings appear and then disappear. Often they reappear for historic, cultural, and social reasons or because of changes in population. These community names, old and new, are possible titles for Alberta ridings. We feel that the names selected could be more representative of the historic and cultural fabric of Alberta.

E.G. Mardon & A.A. Mardon

Chapter 1: Place Names

Names of Alberta

This is a community study of the past and present settlements in the Province of Alberta. Man has inhabited the region for some ten thousand years. However, recorded history only covers the last two hundred years. The place names of Alberta communities reveal the eloquent survival of a succession of races and peoples. The native Amerindians lived a nomadic existence, following the caribou, moose, or bison on their annual migration. In the northern part of the province the Slave, the Beaver, the Chipewyan, and the Sarcee inhabited the woodland and their economy was based on the caribou and moose. To the south wandered the Cree, Blackfoot, Blood, Piegan, Stony and Gros Ventures peoples. They have all contributed their names to physical features in Alberta. It is notable that the names of rivers have the greatest longevity: "Their names are in our rivers and we cannot wash them out."

The first stratum of permanent settlements and onomastics were to be laid down in the last half of the eighteenth century by European explorers and fur-traders. The exploration of the interior of the continent was accomplished largely by water. This was true of Alberta that was approached by way of the Clearwater and the Athabasca Rivers. Within a generation there was a string of fur-trading posts across the northern portion of what is now Alberta. They included Fort of the Forks [1788], Fort George [1792], Fort Edmonton [1795], Fort Vermillion [1788], Rocky Mountain House [1798], Chesterfield House [1800], Fort Dunvegan [1805], Jasper House [1813], and Fort Assiniboine [1825].

These trading posts were fortified. They had heavy outside walls so that invaders could not climb over or set fire to them. These strong walls were usually made of tree trunks set as closely together as possible. At the corners, diagonally opposite each other, square blockhouses were built on top of the walls. The construction of these trading "forts" justified their name, and in several cases, the towns that grew around these early fortified posts have kept the descriptive word "Fort" as part of their name.

The next stratum of permanent settlements owes its existence to Christian missionaries. In 1838, the first two missionaries ever to enter Alberta visited Fort Edmonton. Fathers Francois Blanchet and Modeste Demers, acting on orders from Bishop Provencher of St. Boniface, rested here on their way to open a mission at Fort Vancouver on Columbia River. Two years later, Reb. R.T. Rundle, representing the Wesleyan Society of London, commenced his missionary labours. At the same time Catholic missionaries such as Fr. Thibault, Fr. Lacombe, OMI, Fr. Leduc, and Fr. Petitot, OMI, commenced their work among nomadic Aboriginals. They established permanent missions at Lac Ste. Anne [1842], Fort Chipewyan [1847], Lac La Biche [1853], St. Alberta [1861], and Lady of Peace, Calgary [1873]. Permanent Protestant missions were established at Rocky Mountain House [1841], Pigeon Lake [1847], Whitefish Lake '1859], Pakan [1863], and Moreley [1873].

The American whiskey forts, which were established across Southern Alberta in the late 1860's, had a brief but turbulent life. They had colourful names such as Fort Whoop-up, Stand Off, Slide Out, Robber's Roost, and Whiskey Gap. Their main influence on the development of the region was that they led directly to the formation of the North West Mounted Police. In the summer of 1874, a detachment of North West Mounted Policed arrived on the western prairie, bringing law and order in its wake. Communities grew up around military posts at Fort Macleod, Fort Calgary, For Saskatchewan and Fort Walsh.

The selection of town-sites every ten miles or so was apparently designed to accommodate an agricultural population dependent on horse-drawn vehicles. Railway or postal officials are responsible for the selection of the vast majority of the names of past and present Alberta communities.

In Alberta there are more than 1900 places that have, some time in their history, reached the status of a community.

In the 1972 Highway Map of the province only a total of 770 communities appear. There are other "communities" such as railway stations and hamlets that are too small to be shown on current maps. Each one, however, no matter how humble, had a name, an identity, and a role to play. The object of this study has been to locate these places in time, space, and nomenclature and to preserve their identity for the future. It includes 1,878 entries and a list of 218 name changes. The origins and meaning of each name is given for some 1,700 places, but is unavailable for about 200.

If the names of communities referred to in this book were classified under the categories suggested by George R. Stewart, the percentage figures would be as shown below. However, it must be emphasized that categories and percentage figures used here are necessarily arbitrary because so many names can easily fit into two or more categories.

DESCRIPTIVE NAMES: It would appear the topography of the land has directly or indirectly been responsible for the naming of 12% of the communities in Alberta. Certainly a sampling of these names gives a picture of the province: Grande Prairie, Picture Butte, and Three Hills.

EUPHEMISTIC NAMES: Idealistic names often express the hopes of early settlers. Names such as Success, Patience, Unity, fall into this group, they make up about three percent of the names of communities.

POSSESSIVE NAMES: Though mountains, rivers and lakes are most often named for a natural feature, communities are often names for an early pioneer, the first postmaster or, in the case of railway station, for a minor official. Many names have been applied because of the feeling that some person owned that particular place. They individual may have owned the land on which the community was built or the place may have been referred to originally as, for example, Halcro's and in time the possessive "s" was dropped. Names in this group account for 21% of community names.

COMMEMORATIVE NAMES: These arise by the process of taking an already established name and giving it a new application, for honorific ends.

> Aboriginal names account for 5%
>
> French names account for 3%
>
> Religious names account for 2%
>
> Literary names account for 3%
>
> Prominent Albertans names account for 4%
>
> Prominent Canadian names account for 5%
>
> Prominent English names account for 4%
>
> Transferred names from other parts of Canada account for only a few
>
> Transferred names from the British Isles account for 12%
>
> Transferred names from the United States account 3%
>
> Transferred names from other parts of the world account for 5%

SHIFT NAMES: These are names that are placed upon places by the mere shifting of the specific name of a geographical feature to a nearby community. Thus from Chief Mountain we get the name of a custom post, or from the Red Deer River, we get the name of the city. This category contains 11% of the names of communities in the province. Many of the names in this category could be classified as descriptive.

INCIDENT NAMES: These identify the place by means of some incident, which had occurred at or near it, such as Grizzly Bear, Pincher Creek, or Whiskey Gap. Three percent of names are in this group.

MANUFACTURED NAMES: Neologisms account for about 4% of the names of Alberta communities. Often two names are combined such as Carway, Scotford, and Ukalta, or names are reversed such as Niton and Retlaw.

There is an interesting ethnic pattern discernible throughout the names of communities across Alberta. There are three districts that are predominantly French. They are centered around Falher in the Peace River, Morinville north of the Edmonton and St. Paul – Bonnyville in the northeastern part of the province. The Ukrainian settlement is centered in a wide belt east of Edmonton on both sides of the North Saskatchewan River based on the Mundare and Smoky Lake. German and Scandinavian settlers homesteaded in the Camrose area, in a ring some twenty miles out of the Edmonton, in the Beiseker – Rockyford district northeast of Calgary and in the Lloydminster area, the Barr Colony, Red Deer Valley south to Calgary and on to Fort Macleod.

There is also a religious pattern discernible in Alberta. The French areas are mainly Catholic, the Ukrainian districts are either Orthodox or Catholic, the German-Scandinavian are Lutheran, the English in the Red Deer Valley are Presbyterian, while to the south large numbers of Anglicans are found. There is also a Mormon belt across the southern portion of the province based in Cardston, Raymond, Magrath and Taber. The Mormons introduced irrigated farming. The Metis are concentrated in the Lesser Slave Lake – Athabasca – Cold Lake region. Until recently they were employed in freighting and trapping. These generalizations are taken from the Atlas of Alberta (1969).

Some groups that have settled in the province, such as the Hutterites, have given no place names. This Anabaptist Christian sect rigorously insists on a communal frame of existence, which requires that all important property be shared by the entire community.

Several of the larger ranches that once covered most of southern Alberta are mentioned in this work. The "great days" of the ranchers passed away when large numbers of settlers arrived from eastern Canada, the United States and Europe at the turn of the century.

There is a ribbon of development along the railway line across the prairies. The CPR main line crossed the southern part of the province from Medicine Hat, which used to be in the postal district of Saskatchewan until 1905, to Calgary, on to Banff, to cross the continental divide via the Kicking Horse

Pass which was completed in 1883. A branch line was then constructed to Lethbridge and on to the Crowsnest Pass. Branch lines from these were built into the more remote regions. The Grand Trunk and the Canadian Northern linked Edmonton with the east in 1905. They were continued side by side towards the mountains and eventually crossed the continental divide by way of the Yellowhead Pass. The Main north-south route before the railway was the Fort Macleod – Calgary – Edmonton Trail.

Lethbridge was the cradle of the coal industry in Alberta. The first coal was mined by Nicholas Sheran in the 1880's and mining communities sprang up at Coalhurst, Hardieville, Diamond City, as well as Coalbanks, the name of which was later changed to Lethbridge. At one time 500,000 tons of coal was produced from the Lethbridge mines. All the mines in the area are now closed. The coalmines in the Nordegg region of Central Alberta were also closed down in the late 1950's with the development of the petroleum industry. This is also true of the mines in the Coal Branch District south of Edson. The mines in this region of the Rockies once employed close to 10,000 miners, but are now only ghost communities. The names of these once thriving mining settlements include Cadomin, Coal Valley, Coalspur, Foothills, Leyland, Luscar, Mercoal, Mountain Park, Reco, and Starco. They have disappeared from recent maps. The only district where coal is still being mined is in the Crowsnest and Drumheller areas.

The petroleum industry has given rise to a number of communities. Oil City in Waterton National Park was a thriving community in 1902, but has totally disappeared. Turner Valley and Black Diamond south of Calgary were the center of the oil industry in the 1920's.

Alberta's present prosperity dates from the boring in of the Leduc oil field of 1947. Other communities that are associated with the oil and natural gas industry include Medicine Hat, which according to Kipling has hell for its kitchen, Drayton Valley, Redwater, Rainbow Lake, Viking and Lloydminster.

The History of Place Names in Southern Alberta

The study of names, be they of people, places, or physical features have interested men for centuries. However it has only been in recent times that this study has developed into a recognized science. A proper understanding of our cultural heritage and history can be obtained through the investigation of place names. This is as true of Southern Alberta as any other region of the world.

It has been said that place names are a mirror held up to history. The names given to communities of physical features reflect all the phases of the history of the region. They either originate in them or have been applied subsequently in commemoration of notable events or individuals. They show the ever-changing and shifting interests of the inhabitants of the area, and often even give an indication of the attitudes of the early settlers. There are, as well, place names across southern Alberta which, adopted principally in the period of rapid settlements and development in the first decade of the twentieth century when a large number of names had to be found at short notice, commemorate persons, places and events of little or no permanent significance in the historical development of the region.

The study intends to define various categories by which place names in the region of Alberta south of High River-Bassano-Brooks to the United States border can be organized. The same categories apply to the whole of the province, and the historical development is common, but it is this specific area that concerns this study. Of course, many of the five hundred-odd place names that appear on the survey maps of the area can be placed in more than one category or group. The named features include physical features such as mountains, hills, valleys, or as they are more often known in the region, coulees, streams, rivers, lakes and plains as well as places of human habitation (two in number, Lethbridge and Medicine Hat), towns, villages, post offices, hamlets, railway stations and localities and districts.

Even if Alberta was a latecomer on the historical scene, coming into political existence as a province in 1905, it had a rich heritage of place names. The names of places across Northwestern Plains, which was the historic home of the nomadic Aboriginal tribes who followed herds of bison, are derived from two main sources: English and Amerindian. Other ethnic groups such as the French have provided a certain number of place names over the years.

I. Place Names Derived from Nature

There are a large number of place names that have obtained their nomenclature from natural features and from native flora and fauna. The climatic condition of Southern Alberta range from the almost rainless semi-desert of the Palliser Triangle to the east, to the open ranchlands of the foothills to the west where strong, warm westerly winds known locally as Chinook winds keep the ground snow-free most of the winter, to the alpine climate of the Rocky Mountains. The roof of the North American continent is to be found in the eternal snow and ice of the continental divide from which rivers flow into the Pacific Ocean, the Hudson Bay and the Gulf of Mexico. Thus we have Elbow River, named because of the configuration of this tributary of the South Saskatchewan River; Bow River so called because of the shape of its source lake in the Rockies; Twin Butte after two hills in the neighborhood; Picture Butte due to the great beauty of a single hill nearby. Many Island Lake has scores of islets in it. Mountain View on the way to Waterton National Park has one of the best views of the Rockies. Milk River got its name from the colour of its swift flowing water originating from glaciers south of the border. Grassy Lake is a dried up former lake.

There are innumerable places named for birds and animals, such as Brant, Goose Lake, Horsefly Lake, Fly Lake, Crow Lodge, Crowsnest Pass, Mosquito Creek, Snake Dam, Rattlesnake Lake, Deer Lake, Elkwater Lake, Bear Creek, Beaver Mines Racehorse Pass, White Horse Lake, Wild Horse, Bob Creek, Wolf Creek, and Porcupine Hills. Needless to say the name "Buffalo" appears several times, often in connection with pounds, or cliffs over which the bison were driven in the days before the horse came north from Mexico in the eighteenth century.

Plants and trees have given their share of names. Thus we have Willow Creek, Purple Spring (from the colour of the wild flowers), Cypress Hills, Manyberries Creek, Strawberry Lake, Wild Turnip Hill, Cherry Coulee, Juniper Flats, Cottonwood Creek, Drywood Creek, and Arrowwood Creek.

Settlers applied some of these names as they arrived, whilst others go back many years and might be classified as having origins prior to colonization. In several cases, the modern English name is a translation of the Aboriginal name. Others were given by explorers, most of which worked for one of the large fur trading companies, and later missionaries. Yet more places received their first names from the government surveyors and railway builders. Last to arrive were the white settlers and homesteaders who only started to come west in large numbers at the turn of the century. Their arrival resulted in many names coming into common use that would have better been forgotten.

It is most likely that French voyageurs were the first Europeans to visit this part of the continent. Legardeur St. Pierre's Journal of 1752 contains the first reference to the Montagnes de Roche. The Rocky Mountains seen from the east across the prairies appear as a great mass of rocks.

II. Aboriginal Names

Our original inhabitants, the various Aboriginal tribes of the Blackfoot Confederacy, have contributed a heritage of place names. The name of the largest river in the region, the North Saskatchewan continues to be retained. It is a slightly abbreviated form of the Cree word for fast flowing river. The Blackfoot confederacy dominated the southwestern prairies before the coming of the North West Mounted Police. This confederacy consisted of the Blackfoot, whose name is commonly believed to have reference to the discolouring of their moccasins by the ashes of prairie fires. Loosely allied with them were the Bloods and the Piegans whose name indicates that they have badly dressed robes, and the Sarcee, who originally were slaves of the Blackfoot and were settled along the foothills in the path of Kootenay raiders.

The Blackfoot tribes are the earliest historical occupants of the Canadian prairies. They may have inhabited them for a thousand years or more, or they may have moved onto the plains from the woodlands but a few centuries ago. In either case, they had achieved an elaborate culture based on buffalo hunting, even before they had secured firearms from the fur traders and employed horses. Writing-on-Stone Provincial Park near Milk River contains drawings of horses, men and implements cut deep into a sandstone cliff. These petroglyphs are of uncertain date, thought they may have been drawn in the 18th century. It has been said that it is unfortunate that more Aboriginal names have not survived. Yet, on the other hand, we may be lucky, as the spelling of them would cause all kinds of problems for schoolboys. In actual numbers there are not many Aboriginal names still in use across Southern Alberta. Some of those that are include

Piksko, meaning "foothills" or "rolling hills," Pakowki Lake, descriptive name meaning "bad water", Etzikom, Blackfoot for "valley". Seven Persons which is a literal translation of the Aboriginal name Mesekum, meaning "the land is rich," and Okotoks which means "lots of stones" referring to the ford across Sheep Creek on the Calgary Fort Macleod trail. Medicine Hat is a translation of the Aboriginal name saamis meaning "beard", from its shape when seen from a distance.

There are some names that are translations from various Aboriginal dialects. Bow River may derive its name from the willows along its banks that that some Aboriginal groups used to make their bows. The Belly River may get its name from "belly people" or the Gros Ventres of the French Canadian. However, others argue that these two names are adapted from the French of the early voyageurs who refer to "le beau" (Bow) to the right and "la belle" (Belly) to the left, indicated the right and left hand tributaries of the South Saskatchewan. The Oldman River derives its name from Napi, or the Oldman, who is a hero of the Blackfoot. It was believed that he had supernatural powers. Other names, which possibly are translations, include Watching Hill, Drowning Ford, Massacre Butte, and Dead Lodge Canyon. As we become more aware of our heritage, it is likely that more native names will be resurrected, descriptive as they are of the physical features in this part of the province. High River is descriptive, flowing as it does not in a river valley, but across the top of the prairies.

III. FUR AND WHISKEY TRADERS

The Hudson's Bay Company, founded under royal patronage in 1670, had a monopoly on the fur trade in Rupert's Land that covered most of western Canadian for two hundred years. They were seriously challenged by the North West Company during the Napoleonic period. It was only due to the desire of these two fur-trading companies to outdo each other that what is now Alberta was first explored. Fur trading posts were built in southern Alberta. Nevertheless it is believed that several fur traders and explorers passed through the region, although they left no permanent evidence of their stay.

There is a small portion of southern Alberta that is drained by the Milk River, once deemed France's possession as a result of the Quebec Act. This part of the province has, at one time or another, been part of the possessions of Spain, France, the United States, Britain and Canada.

When in 1869 the Hudson's Bay Company sold Rupert's Land to the Canadian government, the Canadian West became open territory. Free traders from the United States moved into southern Alberta, setting up a series of illegal trading posts, which became known as "Whiskey Forts." These trading posts were established chiefly to sell "fire water" to the First Nations. These traders were based at Fort Benton on the Upper Missouri River, less than 200 miles below the Canadian border. The first trading post was established, in 1868, near modern Lethbridge called Fort Hamilton (later to bear the appropriate appellation of Fort Whoop-up). It was soon followed by the erection of small liquor posts such as Stand-Off, Slide-Out, Kipp, Robber's Roost, Fort Spitzee and Whiskey Gap, north of the international boundary, and immediately east of the Rockies.

With the influence of Hudson's Bay Company removed, the

Montana trade began to spread far northward above the American-Canadian border, as well as eastward to the Cypress Hills. In sheer defiance of the law of Canada, and the United States, brigandage straddled and controlled the border country. Unlimited liquor portended utter ruination of the native population in addition to serious outbreaks of smallpox epidemics. Uninterrupted sale of liquor to the First Nations at very high prices often resulted in bloodshed. An officer sent by the government to examine the conditions reported that the entire North West was "without law, order or security for life and property."

IV. The Coming of Law and Order

The Whiskey Forts with their colourful names had a brief and turbulent life, and their main influence on the development of the region was that they led directly to the formation of the North West Mounted Police.

In the summer of 1874 a detachment of this newly established force arrived on the western plains, bringing law and order in its wake. This force was under the command of Colonel James Farquarson MacLeod. The first winter camp of the North West Mounted Police on the banks of Oldman River was named in honor of him. The coming of MacLeod and his mounted police were able to manage Aboriginal conflict on the prairies. The illegal whiskey trade was also suppressed. The American traders either returned to Montana or remained to become law-abiding citizens, while the First Nations' way of life was fast changing due to the disappearance of vast herds of buffalo. The hamlet Walsh is named after Major James Morro Walsh who was an inspector in the force from 1873 to 1883. Colonol A. Irvine, who succeeded MacLeod as the Commissioner, gave his name to a town south of Medicine Hat.

Prior to the establishment of law and order, a few Christian missionaries had worked among the plain aboriginals. The first of these were Rev. J. Rundle and Father Pierre-Jean De Smet (1801-73) from the United States who travelled through the country. Father De Smet named Saint Mary's River after the Virgin Mary. He himself was honored by his Iroquois guide who named a 8,300 foot peak in the Rockies Roche De Smet. Rundle gave his namesake to a mountain in Banff. Father Alberta Lacombe, OMI, was another dominant figure in the development of the west. He baptized his first Christian near Lethbridge in 1871. His word, in the 1880's was enough to pacify the Blackfoot and win their compliance for the building of the Canadian Pacific Railway across their lands, and his influence kept the Blackfoot confederacy tribes from joining the Northwest Rebellion. Del Bonita may get its name from the French Saint Bonita.

What's in a Name?

V. Surveyors and the Coming of the Iron Horse

British and Canadian government survey parties of the 1850's and 1860's named more physical features in a few years five generations. Captain John Palliser's expedition, which lasted three years from 1857-1860, was charged with exploring the western plains in order to ascertain whether a railway could be built through the Rocky Mountains. The Palliser Triangle in the party was Dr. James Hector and also included Lieutenant Thomas Blakiston. Blakiston was given the job of surveying Waterton Lakes area, which he named in honor of Charles Waterton, famed 18th century British naturalist. Mount Blakiston he named after himself. This officer later broke with Palliser and filed a separate report. He was in favor of using either the North Kootenay Pass or the South Kootenay Pass as the route for the railway across the Rockies. With this in mind, he named Railway River. Blakiston also named the Livingstone Range after the famous African explorer, Gould's Dome after the British naturalist, Mount Rae after the Scottish explorer and Mount Head after the then governor of Canada, Sir Edmund Head.

The British Boundary Commission that mapped the United States-Canada border from Lake of the Woods to the Rockies along the 49th parallel named Mount Anderson, Mount Boswell, Cameron Lake, Mount Darrah, Mount Lyall and Mount Richards— all after members of survey commissions.

This was the time when English gentlemen of fortune were looking for adventure. Men such as Lord Milton, Dr. Cheadle, and the Earl of Southesk travelled across what is now Alberta, naming physical features as they went along. It has been said that everybody in the party, including the cook, received a form of immortality by having some small stream or out-of-the-way mountain named in their honor. Many place names given by such men of adventure honor British scientists and naturalists. Later Dominion Land surveyors confirmed these names.

By the 1870's the buffalo, which had at one time roamed in millions across the open prairie from the headwaters of the Missouri to the banks of the North Saskatchewan, were nearly exrinct. This and disease wiped out some Aboriginal peoples' nomadic way of life. They were forced to give up their nomadic habits and adopt of a more sedentary existence. But still a greater economic change was at hand. Through the coming of the railway, hunters and traders were replaced by ranchers and farmers. The building of the Canadian Pacific Railway opened up the prairies to homesteaders and settlers. Railway officials encouraged permanent settlement to pay for the vast construction costs. It has been said that the CPR should make a statue in honor of Louis Riel who lead the Metis and other Aboriginal groups to rebel in 1885, forcing Prime Minister John A. Macdonald to bail out towns along the railway line. Towns which included Magrath (after A. Magrath, MP, first mayor of Lethbridge and a business associate of Sir Alexander Galt); Nanton (after Sir Augustus Nanton, CPR Winnipeg director); Shaughnessy (another associate of Galt); and Warner (after A. L. Warner, land agent for the Alberta railway).

There are at least a score of villages and railway stations also named after railway officials. One interesting example involves the village of Burdett and Coutts. These two communities are named in honor of Baroness Georgina Burdett-Coutts, who was born in 1814 and was said to be the richest heiress in all of England. In 1881 she married an American 37 years her junior. Her wealth opened up and developed coal mining. The former name of this community was Woodpecker— a joking reference to an old CPR boxcar, which was for years used as a telegraph office.

Other names that must be included in this list are Bain (after a section foreman); Dunmore (after CPR shareholder Lore Dunmore); Fincastle (one of Lord Dunmore's titles); Iddesleigh (after Lord Iddesleigh); Stirling (a minor railway official); Suffield (after Baron Suffield, a CPR shareholder); and Woodhouse (another minor railway official).

One some lines, as map-readers have observed, railway officials employed the device of naming stations in a certain order. One such series in neighboring Saskatchewan ends with Vera, Winter, Yonker, and Zumbro. Winter was the name of the contractor of that section, Vera was his daughter and Zumbro was his dog! An example of this in southern Alberta involves Retlaw. It is Walter in reverse, named after Walter Baker, private secretary to the Earl of Dufferin, then the Governor General of Canada. The other station on this branch line was also to spell Retlaw or Walter backwards: Retlaw, Enchant, Travers, Lomond, Armada and Winfield, a mere water tower siding beyond Armada. Another branch line running north of Brooks boasts of Bassano, Countess, Rosemary, Duchess, Millicent, Patricia and Empress. Countess refers to the Countess of Bassano, Rosemary to the daughter of the Duke of Sutherland, Duchess to his wife, Lady Millicent, Patricia to the daughter of the Duke of Connaught, then Governor General of Canada, and Empress to Queen Victoria, among whose titles was Empress of India.

SETTLERS

Countless place names originate with pioneer settlers who chose names of post offices, school districts and rural municipalities. Ethnic and religious group settlements, colonization companies and their leaders contributed or were honored in this fashion. The strong influence of the Cardston (after Charles Ora Card), Franksburg (after Christopher Frank); Leavitt (after William Leavitt), Orton (after Josiah Orr), Raymond (after Raymond Knight, and Taber (after the American senator Tabor of Colorado). There are cases of conflicting stories concerning the origin of a certain place name. Taber is an example. The Geographic Board of Canada's Place-Names of Alberta, published in 1928, states that it received its name from the first part of the word "tabernacle". This was out of consideration for the Mormon settlers in the district. The next station on the rail line is Elcan ("nacle" spelled backwards).

Some early settlers and homesteaders applied the name of communities of places they had known or had come from. Thus we have Aden (Arabia), Aetna (Italy), Brocket (after the English estate of Lord Mount Stephen), Cluny (Scotland), Lomond (Scotland), New Dayton (Ohio), Scandia (Scandinavian settlement), St. Kilda (Scotland), and Wrentham (England). Occasionally the aspiration of the pioneers can be seen in the names they gave their communities. Examples that come to mind are Faith, Hope, Charity (later changed to Charles on the request of the inhabitants), Lucky, Strike, Bad Land Hills, Easy Coulee, Tough Coulee and Success.

Among communities named for individual settlers, many were those of the first postmaster in the particular district. Thus we have: Burmis named after two residents, Burns and Kemmis, Carmangay after C.W. Carman and his wife née Gay, Champion, a former Winnipeg banker, Fallow after A. Halkett's wife's maiden name, Kimball an early homesteader, Herronton after an original member of the N.W.M.P. John Herron, Lundbreck a compound of Lund and Breckenridge, operators of a local sawmill Lee Creek— W.S. Lee was an early settler, McGregor Lake, an early settler, Milo named after the postmaster, "Milo Munroe". Nobleford after Charles Noble who perfected farm machinery, Oyen, an early Scandinavian settler, Parkland after an old resident of Park Hill, Schuler after the postmaster, Shouldice after James Shouldice, owner of the town site, Stimson, a wealthy rancher, Todd, an early settler and Willing after Horace Willing, a local farmer.

Among the last regions of this part of the province to receive names are the mountain peaks north of United States border. The Geographic Board of Canada in 1917 approved a large list of names connected with persons or events of the Great War. They include the naming of peaks after King Albert and Queen Elizabeth of Belgium, and after Baston de Leval, Gelgian lawyer who defended Edith Cavell. Famous soldiers and sailors of the allies were commemorated by the following mountain names: British— Allenby, Beatty, Birdwood, Cornwell, French, Haigh, Jellicoe, Maude, Monro, Robertson, Sir Douglas (Haig), Smuts and Tyrwhitt. French— Castelnan, Condonnier, Roch, Joffre, Lyantey, Mangin, Nivelle, Petain, and Sarrail, Italian— Abruzzi, Aosta, and Cadorna, Russian— Brussilof, Serbian— Putnik, and Belgian— Leman.

The names of eminent Canadian soldiers who fought in the Great War were bestowed upon peaks as follows: Bishop, Burstall, Byng, Currie, Lipsett, Macdonnell, Mercer, Morrison, Turner and Watson. Other features were named after places where Canadians fought: Festubert, Gravenstafel, La Couotte, St. Eloi, Flanders, Hollebeke, Langemarck, Scarpe, Somme and Vimy Ridge. The battle to Jutland, the greatest naval battle of the war, is commemorated by peaks bearing the names of sunken British warships: Indefatigable, Inflexible, Invincible, Black Prince, Chester, Cornwall, Fortune, Marlborough, Nestor, Shark, Turbulent and Warrior.

There are three names of Latin origin: Granum, meaning grain, Juno, one of the Roman female deities, and Vulcan, the god of fire. There are three communities that can boast of their literary origins: Blackie named in honor of a Scottish author, Conrad named after Joseph Conrad, the popular novelist, and Mazeppa after the Cossack hetman, hero of Lord Byron's poem Mazeppa.

Another category of place names is made up of those formed by the combination of manipulation of words and names. Retlaw is an example that we have already mentioned. Others include: Comrey, formed from the initial letters of the names of the following early homesteaders: Columbus Larson, Ole Roen, Mons Roen, R. Rolson, J. J. Evenson and Ed Yager, Maleb, a combination of the initials of the names of Morley Bowen— Morley, Amy, Lorne, Elizabeth, Bowen. Maybutt after May Butt who married Mr. Fisher, owner of the original town site. The naming of the town of Legend has nothing to do myths but was originally written as two words "leg" and "end", indicating the end of the branch line. County of Forty Mile, refers to the fact that there is a coulee in the district which is forty miles in length.

It could be early to make up a category of place names which reflect humorous stories, although it may not be possible to verify the stories. One of these related to Pincher Creek; allegedly a pair of horseshoe pincers were lost in the stream and the travellers had to homestead there. Readymade, Alberta, derived its name when railway officials built a house on each quarter section before the arrival of the first settlers. Turin is said to be named after an imported Percheron stallion, which eight local farmers came together to buy. Foremost is the farthest point the railway reached before the company went broke! The Bear's Hump, overlooking Waterton town, is all that is left of Bear Mountain, which was changed to Crandall. Dish Pan Lake is where some plates fell to the bottom and could not be recovered. Cowley may have gotten its name from the opening lines of Thomas Gray's "Elegy Written in a Country Churchyard" which came to the mind of F.W. Godsal, a local rancher while he was watching his cattle grazing across the open prairie:

> The curfew tolls the knell of parting day,
>
> The lowing herd wind slowly o'er the lea.

PLACE NAMES TODAY

It is interesting to note that the Dominion Census of 1941 revealed that in Alberta sixty percent of the population were rural dwellers and forty percent lived in urban areas. Twenty years later, the figures were reversed; the 1961 census shows that forty percent were rural and sixty percent urban. The trend is continuing as rural communities wither and die. The railways have closed down hundreds of stations on branch lines across the province and are discontinuing service. Service areas are increasing in size because people are more inclined to travel by car than by horse and buggy. Rural and village schools are closing as the service areas increase in size. Now children are bussed to one central school from a fifty-mile radius. Young children now often spend two hours a day on a bus. This means that towns are becoming villages and villages are becoming hamlets or merely localities. Some one hundred post offices in the Edmonton region were closed down last year. The place names of Alberta are starting to disappear.

We are witnessing a change in our way of life and our civilization. Without any history, without an understanding of the past, we lose our sense of value; everything becomes of equal importance. I believe without family and local loyalty, there is no chance of national loyalty. As it has been said, if you don't love your wife and family, it is no used talking about loving mankind.

G.K. Chesterton, the British Man of Letters, put it thus:

> The chapels and the villas
>
> Where I learnt with little labour,
>
> The ways too love my fellow-man,
>
> And hate my next door neighbor.

In Alberta today we are witnessing the growth of the two metropolitan areas of Edmonton and Calgary at a rate of close to two thousand a month— the countryside is being depopulated. Some ten farmers close their front door for the last time every week.

The land is being farmed in larger and larger units. It reminds one of the later Roman Empire when a few slaves worked vast estates. What will happen? Possibly new barbarians will again occupy the vast prairies. But let us understand our place names- let us understand our history. For the stories behind the place names of Alberta record history as colourful, picturesque and varied as any tale that has ever been told.

Names of Alberta

Alberta

~most westerly of the three prairie provinces.

It has an area of some 255,000 square miles. Its average width from west to east is more than 300 miles, its length 800 miles from the 49th parallel to the border of the Northwest Territories. It owes its name to H.R.H. Princess Louis Caroline Alberta, fourth daughter of Queen Victories and wife of the Marquis of Lorne (later Duke of Argyle), who served as Governor-General of the Dominion of Canada from 1878 to 1883. She died in 1939 at 91 years of age. He chose his wife's name for the new postal district created in the Northwest Territories in 1882, Northern Alberta was the postal district of Athabasca.

Athabasca

~town north of Edmonton

Known also as ATHABASCA LANDING, it is located on the Athabasca River where the Hudson's Bay Company established a post in 1883. The Cree name means, "where there are reeds".

Banff

~town site in Banff National Park

This community was named by Lord Strathcona after a town near his birthplace in Scotland. The Scottish namesake is the capital of the country of the same name, and was the site of a royal castle that on three occasions was the headquarters of King Edward I of England during his attempts to conquer Scotland in the thirteenth century. The Gaelic word bunaimb, "the mouth of the river", has been corrupted into "Banff". According to Mrs. C. M. Matthews, its original form was banba, a term of endearment meaning "little pig".

Beaumont

~town south of Edmonton

Early French Canadian pioneer settlers named it in 1895 because of the beauty of the locality. It is located on a hill with a view of the North Saskatchewan River. The name is French for "beautiful mountain".

The population was 234 in 1972 and increased to 5,685 in 1997. It is now a city dormitory community.

Beaver Mines

~hamlet southwest of Pincher Creek

The Beaver coalmines are located here. The post office was opened in 1912.

Beaver River

~former station northeast of Bonnyville

It is named after a nearby river. The post office is now called Le Goff

Beaver Dam

~hamlet southwest of Pincher Creek

The name of this small animal appears twenty-eight times on the map of Alberta.

Beaverhill

~former station north of Beaverhill Lake

The name for the nearby hills was first used on the Thompson Map in 1814.

Beaverlodge

~town west of Bear Lake

The Beaver coalmines are located here. The post office was opened in 1912.

Crowfoot

~hamlet east of Calgary

It was named in honor of Crowfoot, head chief of the Blackfoot Nation, at the signing of the Treaty Number Seven at Blackfoot Crossing on the Bow River in 1877.

When Sitting Bull crossed the border into Canada after annihilating General Custer's forces at Little Big Horn, Crowfoot refused to join him in further battles. This peace-loving chief, who had survived nineteen battles himself, persuaded the Blackfoot Confederacy to join Louis Riel in his ill-fated uprising in 1885.

Calgary

~the largest city in the province, situated at the junction of the Bow and Elbow Rivers within sight of the Rocky Mountains.

It is believed to be on or near the site of FORT LA JOHNQUIERRE which was built by La Vérandrye in 1757 and abandoned the next year. FORT BRISEBOISE, a North West Mounted Police outpost from FORT MACLEOD, was erected in 1875, and renamed FORT CALGARY in 1876. That year Assistant Commissioner A. G. Irvine wrote to

Ottawa as follows:

> As we now have a post of Fort at Bow River, it would be well if it were known by some name...Colonel Macleod has suggested the name of Calgary, which I believe, is Scotch, means clear running water, a very appropriate name, I think.

Mrs. C.M. Mathews in Place Names of the English-Speaking World (1972) says: "It was probably given by Norsemen, for all those islands (Hebridean) were once part of a Viking Kingdom, and it may have meant an enclosure for calves."

Calgary also happened to be the name of the ancestral estate of Colonel Macleod's cousins, the Mackenzie's of the Isle of Mull, Scotland, which he had visited shortly before coming to western Canada. Edward Blake, the federal Minister of Justice at the time, approved of Irvine's suggestion concerning the name of the future city. The Hudson's Bay Company opened a trading station here in 1876 with Angus Fraser in charge.

In 1883, a post office was opened in the same year the Canadian Pacific Railway came to town, with a population of 500. It became a city in 1893. The famous Calgary Stampede was inaugurated in 1912.

The population was 398,034 in 1972 and increased to 780,000 in 1997. (See: Bowness; Forest Lawn; Glenbow; Priddis)

Calgary-Edmonton Trail

Staging Posts (1883-1891)

When the Canadian Pacific Railway tracks reached Calgary in the autumn of 1883, the Edmonton mail route changed from the 1,000 mile Winnipeg-Fort Carlton-Edmonton to the 200 mile Calgary-Edmonton Trail. A one-way ticket cost twenty-five dollars and the journey took approximately seven days. The stage had to be ferried across the Bow River to the Nose Hill side. During fall freeze-up and the spring thaw, there was no stagecoach. This was the means of travel for eight years until the Calgary-Edmonton railway tracks reached Strathcona, across the river from Edmonton 1891. When the railway became operational, the time for the journey was cut to 12 hours.

Dickenson Stopping House

~on McPherson Creek at mile 18 of the trail north of Calgary

The proprietor was Captain Francis. J. Dickens, former member of the N.W.M.P. He was a son of Charles Dickens, the British novelist and author of A Tale of Two Cities.

Scarlet'S Stopping House

~ at Service Berry Creek Crossing mile 35 of the trail

The proprietor was Samuel T. Scarlet, an American squatter who had arrived in 1872. In 1909 he was an unsuccessful Legislature candidate.

Lone Pine Stopping House

~at mile 63 of the trail

For several years the proprietor was "Paddy", a French Canadian Métis.

Travelers referred to his establishment as "Hotel Rustle". The visitors were required to rustle up their own lay beds, look after the stagecoach's four houses, and to cook their own meals.

Red Deer Crossing

~at mile 93 of the road

The proprietor was William Bannerman, a Scot and former Member of Parliament. He opened a post office and obtained an "official ferry license". He operated a large scow to transport the coach across the wide river.

(See: Red Deer)

Whitford Stopping House

~at Blindman's River crossing mile 100 on the trail

The proprietor was Charles Whitford, a prominent pioneer settler. A constituency was named after him.

(See: WHITFORD)

Barnett's Stopping House

~at mile 115 on the trail

The proprietor was Edward Barnett, former member of the N.W.M.P. who was one of the original homesteaders on the Strawberry Plain.

(See: LACOMBE)

Barker's Stopping House

~at Battle River Crossing, mile 125 on the trail

(See: PONOKA)

Telford's Stopping House

~at mile 187 on the trail

The proprietor was Robert T. Telford, former member of the N.W.M.P. Later he sat in the Alberta Legislature from 1905 to 1913. It was a steamboat landing below Strathcona in the south side of the valley of the North Saskatchewan River where the trail ended. Edmonton was located on the north bank.

(See: LEDUC)

Castor

~town east of Red Deer

The Latin word "castor" means "beaver". This name was probably suggested by the name of Beaverdam River that runs through the community. Beavers were still plentiful in the area as late as 1921. The post office was opened in 1909.

The population in 1972 was 1,103. It declined to 933 by 1998.

Cochrane Ranch
~west of Calgary

It was the first large ranch to be established by Senator Cochrane in Alberta. It received a federal charter in May 1881, giving it rights to 109,000 acres of grassland. It was sold to the Mormon Church in 1906.

Drumheller
~city, former coalmining community

It was named after Samuel Drumheller, the proprietor of several large coalmines in the district. He was born in Walla Walla, State of Washington, in 1864, and came north to Canada with a herd of cattle. Drumheller bought the town site in 1910 from Thomas P. Greentree, the original homesteader. His name was given to the post office, which opened in 1911. Rail service dates from 1912. DRUMHELLER was incorporated as a village in 1913, as a town in 1916 and as a city in 1930. It is described thus:

> [A] veritable twentieth century Midas, everything that he undertakes brings in a rich return, and as controller of vast financial interests in the province, Drumheller exercises a tremendous influence on its industrial life.

The population in 1972 was 5,240. It increased to 6277 by 1998.

Edmonton
~capital city of the Province of Alberta

Lovell's Gazetteer of British North America, published in 1872, states that:

Edmonton is a fortified village in the Northwest Territories in Lat. 53°33' Long. 113°28' west built of red earth, enclosed by high pickets, and entered battlemented gateway. Its vicinity is rich in coal and gold and other minerals.

It took its name from FORT EDMONTON that was built in 1795, twenty miles farther down the North Saskatchewan River, by George Sutherland, of the Hudson's Bay Company. It was named after Edmonton, near London, England probably as a compliment to John Prudens, Sutherland's who was born there. This fort was destroyed by First Nation invaders in 1807. A new fort of the same name was built in 1808 on the slope of the high bank within the limits of the present city EDMONTON. Later, the word "Fort" fell into disuse and the first post office was opened on February 1, 1877, it was named simply, EDMONTON.

Edson

~town west of Edmonton

It was named after Edson Chamberlain, an official of the Grand Trunk Pacific Railway, which reached this point in 1910. The community was first called HEATHERWOOD.

The population was 4,051 in 1972 and increased to 7,400 in 1998.

Fort Saskatchewan

~city northeast of Edmonton

It is the site of the first North West Mounted Police north of CALGARY which was built in 1875. The residents of EDMONTON were expected to move down river and the area was initially occupied by foresighted police. Saskatchewan is the Cree word for "swift current".

The population was 5,734 in 1972 and increased to 12,400 in 1997.

Grande Prairie

~city in the Peace River Community

The name is the French for "large plain", and was given in 1912 by Bishop Grouard, OMI, the Catholic missionary who described the region of gently undulating grass as "la grande prairie". This name eventually found its way into government reports.

The population was 12,054 in 1972 and increased to 29,242 in 1997.

Fort Macleod
~first N.W.M.P. Post on the Western Prairie

It was named in honor of Colonel James Farquhar Macleod (1832-1894), the commander of the first force of the North West Mounted Police to arrive in what is now Alberta. In the 1870's he brought law and order to the western prairies, and negotiated the historic Treaty Seven with the Blackfoot, Sarcee and Nakoda. Upon his retirement from the force, Macleod was appointed a magistrate, and then a judge. In Blackfoot stamix-otokan-okowy means "bull's home", Colonel Macleod being known as "Bull's head" because he had a buffalo head over the door of his residence. The crest of the clan Macleod of Skye is a bull's head.

The population was 2,750 in 1972 and increased to 3,112 in 1997.

Fort McMurray
~city on the Athabasca River at the junction of the Clearwater River

It is located at the foot of a ninety-mile stretch of rapids on the Athabasca and the beginning of a course navigable north to the Mackenzie River, making it an important transshipping center. Settlement at the location began with a trading post established by the North West Company in 1788 called FORT OF THE BORKS. David Thompson descended the Athabasca River in 1799 and arrived here. The post was taken over by the Hudson's Bay Company in 1821, rebuilt in 1870 by Factor H. J. Moberly. It was renamed FORT MCMURRAY in honor of William McMurray (died 1877), Chief Factor of the fur trading company who was in charge of Isle of the Cross about that time. That settlement was incorporated into the town in 1947.

The population was 6,681 in 1972 and increased to 34,000 in 1997.

Hardisty

~former town south of Edmonton

This central Alberta community was named in 1906 after Senator Richard Hardisty (1831-1889), who was for many years chief factor of the EDMONTON district of the Hudson's Bay Company. Born at a trading post on Lake Nipissing, young Hardisty followed in his father's footsteps and joined the Hudson's Bay Company. In time, he was appointed inspecting chief factor for the northern department. He was called to the Canadian Senate by Prime Minister John A. Macdonald as the first Senator for the district of Alberta. He was drowned in an accident while travelling from Prince Alberta to Qu'Appelle by wagon. His niece's husband was senator Sir James Lougheed.

The population was 626 in 1972 and increased to 656 in 1997.

Jasper

~town west of Edmonton, in Jasper National Park

It was named after Jasper House, which was a North West Company's trading post in charge of Jasper Hawes, in 1817. The post was in existence in 1814 when François Decoigne was in charge. Its surrounding area was set aside in 1907 by the federal government for the perpetual use, benefit and enjoyment of the people. It contains 4,000 square miles, and is the largest of the fourteen federal reservations for park purposes. It is historic ground, many early explorers having passed this way to the Pacific, among them Alexander Mackenzie, David Thompson and Simon Fraser.

(See: DECOIGNE)

Leduc

~city south of Edmonton

It was named in 1890 to honor Father Hippolyte Leduc, OMI. Father Leduc was a French-born Oblate missionary who worked for more than fifty years among Aboriginals as a missionary on the western prairie. The discovery of an oil field west of the town in 1947 introduced an oil boom that is still continuing. Leduc today is part of the greater Edmonton area; there is almost no open farmland undeveloped land between the two cities.

The population was 4,070 in 1972 and increased to 14,117 in 1997.

(See: CALGARY-EDMONTON TRAIL STAGING POSTS; TELFORD)

Lethbridge
~the third largest city in Alberta

It was named in honor of William Lethbridge (1824-1901), who was the first President of the North West Coal and Navigation Company. Lethbridge was a British financier who was persuaded to invest his money in the development of the coal deposits along the banks of the Oldman River by Sir Alexander Galt. Prior to 1885, the community was called COALBANKS. This name in Cree is achsaysim, or "steep banks". The province's third University was opened here in 1967.

Medicine Hat
~city in southeastern Alberta

The site of the present city is so called in the report the North West Mounted Police for 1882 and about this year the first house was erected. Medicine Hat is a translation of the Blackfoot name saamis, meaning "head-dress of a medicine man".

One of the many explanations connected with the name was a fight between the Cree and Blackfoot tribes. When the Cree medicine man was fleeing, he lost his war bonnet in the river. Another connects the origin of the name with the slaughter of a party of settlers in the early days and the hat was worn by one of the victims. Yet another story states that the name is applied originally to a hill east of the city, resembling the shape of Aboriginal head-gear for a medicine man. This hill is styled Medicine Hat on a map of the Department of the Interior dated 1883.

Nose Hill Ranch

~west of Calgary, now part of the city

The proprietor was Thomas Riley (1842-1913). He came west with his seven songs in 1888. He was a pioneer rancher. Two of his songs, Ezra H. Riley and Harold W. H. Riley served in the Legislature, and his grandson, Justice Harold Riley served for many years as an Alberta Supreme Court Trial Division Judge.

Peace River

~town in Peace River Country

The Peace River Country extends across a large section of Northern Alberta between the fifty-fourth and fifty-ninth parallel. The soil of this region is similar to that parkland along the banks of the North Saskatchewan River with an annual rainfall of about fifteen inches. Despite its northern latitude, the area is blessed with an average temperature range that assures normal harvests. The town of PEACE RIVER is located at the junction of the Peace and Little Smoky Rivers. Before 1919 the community was called PEACE RIVER CROSSING ST. MARY'S HOUSE, the first Hudson's Bay Company trading post to be built in the Peace River Country in 1818, was located near here.

The population was 5,384 in 1972 and increased to 6,696 in 1997.

Peace Point

~locality on the north shore of the Peace River

In the account of his voyage to the Pacific in 1792-1793 Alexander Mackenzie narrates that he entered the Peace River on October 12, and continues:

> On the 13th noon we came to Peace Point, from which, according to the report of my interpreter, the river derives its name; it was the spot where the Knistenaux (Crees) and Beaver tribe settled their disputes, the real name of the river and point being that of the land which was the object of contention. When

this country was invaded by the Knistenaux, they found the Beaver tribe inhabiting the lands, and the adjoining tribes were those they called Slaver. They drove both these tribes before them, the latter proceeded down the river from Lake of the Hill (Lake Athabasca) in consequence of which that part of it obtained the name of Slave River. The former proceeded up the river; and when the Knistenaux made peace with them, this place was settled to be the boundary.

Red Deer

~city halfway between Calgary and Edmonton

It was named after the Red Deer River that flows east across central Alberta. The name is a translation of the Cree was-ka-sioo. Three miles west of the present city is a ford where the trail from the south to Edmonton crosses the river. Traffic north over the prairie greatly increased after the Canadian Pacific Railway reached Calgary in 1883, and in the autumn of that year, a stopping place and trading post was erected at the RED DEER CROSSING. As time passed the word "crossing" dropped out of use. In 1884, a post office was opened. In 1891, the railway line reached the Red Deer River original settlement and after debate, it was agreed that the name RED DEER would be retained.

The population was 27,431 in 1972 and increased to 59,826 in 1997.

Rosebud

~hamlet southwest of Drumheller

It was so named in 1896. It derives its name from the Blackfoot name of the river which was okokiniskway, meaning "many rose buds". This is the Edge Coal Creek where Peter Fidler noticed coal in 1792, and was referred to as Edge Creek by Dr. James Hector in 1859.

St. Alberta

~incorporated city now surrounded by Edmonton

Bishop Taché of St. Boniface, Manitoba, named it in 1861, after St. Albert of Louvain. It was at St. Albert, where the Sturgeon River winds its way through a valley of poplar pine trees, that Father Lacombe built the first bridge of any size west of the Great Lakes in 1863. It is the location of Alberta's fourth degree-granting institution of higher learning, the University of Athabasca.

The population was 11,249 in 1972 and increased to 22,195 in 1997.

St. Paul

~town northeast of Edmonton

Father Lacombe, a missionary, who in 1894 obtained four townships for a metis settlement, founded this community. He called it ST. PAUL DES METIS. After twelve years the project was abandoned and settlement was opened to other settlers. The village of ST. PAUL DES METIS was incorporated in 1912 and was reached by the railway service in 1920.

The population was 4,241 in 1972 and increased to 5,021 in 1997.

Sherwood Park

~former post office east of Edmonton, now part of the city

It was developed in the 1950's as a dormitory town for Edmonton. The school is called "Robin Hood".

The population in 1972 was 14,282.

(See: CAMPBELL TOWN)

Strathcona

~former city on the south bank of the North Saskatchewan River opposite Edmonton, and now a suburb of Edmonton.

It was established in 1899 but was annexed to the city of Edmonton in 1911. It was named in honor of Donald Smith, Lord Strathcona and Mount Royal (1820-1914). Born in Scotland, he entered the service of the Hudson's Bay Company in 1837. While still one of the Company's traders in Labrador, Smith began to buy stock in both the Hudson's Bay Company and the Bank of Montreal. In 1869 Smith became head of the Hudson's Bay Company, Montreal department, and in 1871 a Member of Parliament.

With his financial interests widening, he became a railway magnate and one of the men chiefly responsible for the building of the Canadian Pacific Railway across the continent. In 1886 he was knighted. Three years later he became governor of the Hudson's Bay Company, a post that he held until his death. In 1896 he was appointed Canada's High Commissioner in the United Kingdom, and the next year he acquired the title of Lord Strathcona and Mount Royal. An extremely wealthy man, Lord Strathcona raised a regiment, Lord Strathcona's Horse, for service in the South African War. It was also the name at one time of a federal riding.

Telford

~south of Edmonton

It was named after Robert T. Telford (1860-1932) who served with the Northwest Mounted Police as a young man. He became the first pioneer settler in the community later named after him and served as Mayor. Robert Telford also served in the Legislature from 1905-1913. The name was changed in 1905.

(See: LEDUC; CALGARY-EDMONTON TRAIL STAGING POSTS, TELFORD'S STOPPING HOUSE)

Vegreville

~town east of Edmonton

This town was first settled in 1895 by French-speaking Catholic pioneers from the State of Kansas. The post office, which was opened that year, was named in honor of Father Valentin Végréville who was taken prisoner by Louis Riel at Batoche in 1885, but was later released. He died in 1903.

The population was 3,776 in 1972 and increased to 5,138 in 1997.

Wetaskiwin

~city on the old Calgary-Edmonton trail

The eighth largest city in Alberta, it came into being circa 1892 when the Calgary and Edmonton Railway was being constructed. The Cree name for the neighboring Peace Hill, Wetaskiwin, was adopted. The name derives from the word wi-taski-oo-cha-ka-tin-ow. According to C.D. Smith, the Cree and the Blackfoot made a treaty here in 1867, after an exhausting battle.

The population was 6,586 in 1972 and increased to 10,771 in 1997.

Yellowhead

~former station west of Jasper

It is named after the nearby pass across the Rockies. The Yellowhead Pass immortalizes the Iroquois-Metis trapper of the early nineteenth century, who was nicknamed "Tête Jaune" or "Yellowhead". He may have been François Decoigne who was employed by the Hudson's Bay Company in 1814, and cached furs in the vicinity; or Pierre Hatsinaton, who guided a party of Iroquois fur hunters in the area in 1820.

(See: DECOIGNE)

What's in a Name?

What's in a Name?

All history resolves itself very easily into the biographies of a few stout and earnest persons.

-Ralph Waldo Emerson (1803-1882)

Chapter Two: Biographies

Elective Representatives From Alberta

The House of Commons

The House of Commons is the real centre of parliamentary authority and exercises a preponderant influence in the government. It is the organized medium through which the public finds expression and exercises its ultimate political power. It forms the indispensable part of the legislature and it is the body to which the executive must turn for justification and approval. It is based on popular election and, basically, representation by population determines the number of seats allotted to each province, with provision for adjustment after each decennial census.

The Early Years 1905-1921

When Alberta was created by act of Parliament, it was sending four members to Ottawa: two Conservatives and two Liberals. In 1908 the province's representation was increased to seven: three were Conservatives and four were Liberals. In the 1911 general election that saw Robert Borden and the Conservatives take power for the first time in fifteen years. Alberta did not match up with the rest of Canada. It sent six Liberals to Ottawa, and the only Conservative was R.B. Bennett, the Calgary lawyer who was to become the Prime Minister of Canada some twenty years later.

In the war-time election of 1917, Alberta sent a total of eleven supporters of Borden's national government to Ottawa. Only one Laurier Liberal was selected.

The Reign of the United Farmers of Alberta 1921-1935

In the 1921 federal election the United Farmers of Alberta and their allies were successful in capturing all the ridings. It was the first time that Alberta turned her back on the old-line parties. It was not until thirty-seven years later when John Diefenbaker, a prairie lawyer, was the leader of the Progressive Conservative party, that voters again cast their ballots in a significant number for either the Conservatives or Liberals. In the federal elections in 1925, 1926, and 1930, the rural areas of the province remained faithful to Henry Wise Wood's agrarian protest movement.

Members of the House of Commons Elected From Alberta Constituencies (1905-1972)

Herbert Bealey Adshead
Independent Labour for Calgary East 1926-1930

Born near Manchester, England, in 1862, he was educated at Manchester Grammar School. He came to Canada in 1878 and four years later married Ellen S. Unwin of Madoc, Ontario, a relative of the Unwin Brothers who were Publishers of London, England. He obtained a teaching certificate from the Ottawa normal school and taught for several years near Olds, Alberta, while homesteading at the same time. Finally he rented his farm in 1912 and moved to Calgary, where he entered civic politics. He was elected to the city council four times, and in 1917 he was defeated in his attempt to become the mayor by only ten votes. He stood for the Legislature as an Independent farmer in 1921, but was defeated. His political affiliation changed from Liberal to right-wing Labor. He was elected for Calgary East in the federal election of 1926 as aLabourcandidate and represented Calgary for four years in Ottawa. He died May 1932. Religion: United Church.

Patrick Harvey Ashby
Social Credit for Edmonton East 1945-1949

Born in Sussex, England, in 1890, he was the son of Frederick Ashby, a Brit. He was educated at private schools in England, at Wadham College, Oxford, and at the University of Alberta. He came to Canada at the age of fifteen. Ashby became a successful farmer and rancher in the Edmonton district. He served in the Canadian army during the Great War. He became active in federal politics when he ran as a Social Credit candidate in 1945 for the urban riding of Edmonton East. He won the election and served one term in the Commons. Religion: Anglican.

Gerald William Baldwin

Progressive Conservative for Peace River 1958-1980

Born at Palmerston, New Zealand, in 1907, he was the son of Vaudrey Baldwin, who was of British descent. Coming to Canada as a child, he was educated at Edmonton and the University of Alberta. He has been named a Q.C. and a bencher of the Alberta Law Society. He has been interested in politics all his life. He first ran as a Conservative in the provincial election of 1935 that saw William Aberhart's Social Crediters come to power. He was defeated. He ran again as a Conservative federally in 1957 with no better luck. Baldwin was first elected in the Diefenbaker sweep of 1958. He has held the large northern Alberta riding since. In the last federal election he had a 7,000-odd-vote majority. He was named House leader of the Conservative group in the House of Commons. In 1985 he was named an Officer of the Order of Canada. Religion: Anglican.

Harold Raymond Ballard

Progressive Conservative for Calgary South 1965-1968

Born at Provost, Alberta, in 1918, he is the son of William Ballard and Mable Armstrong, both of British descent. He was educated at Lloydminster and the University of British Columbia where he received a Bachelor of Arts and a Bachelor of Commerce degree. Ballard was a Calgary chartered accountant. He became interested in civic politics in the 1960's and served four years as a Calgary alderman (1962-1966) before he moved into federal politics. He was the Progressive Conservative candidate in Calgary South in the 1965 general election. He won the seat by a narrow margin of 155 votes. Three years later Liberal Patrick Mahoney, later named to Trudeau's cabinet in 1972 as the Minister of State, defeated him. Religion: Anglican.

Richard Bedford Bennett

MLA for the N.W.T. 1898-1905

Conservative MLA for Calgary 1909-1911

Conservative for Calgary 1911-1917, 1925-1938

Minister of Justice 1921

Minister of Finance 1926

Prime Minister of Canada 1930-1935

Leader of the Opposition 1935-1938

Born at Hopewell, New Brunswick, in 1870, he was on both his father's and his mother's side of the ninth generation born in North America. His father's ancestors were of United Empire Loyalist stock while his mother's people came directly to Canada in 1760. He was educated at public school in New Brunswick and at Dalhousie University, Halifax, where he obtained a law degree. He was called to the New Brunswick Bar in 1893 and started to practice law in Chatham with L.J. Tweddie as his partner. Senator James Lougheed persuaded him to join his Calgary firm. Bennett, who became a very wealthy man and never married, was always interested in politics. He was elected to the Regina Legislature of the Northwest Territories, the Alberta Legislature (1909-1911) and the House of Commons (1911-1917 and 1935-1938). He served in Arthur Meighen's first cabinet in 1921 as Minister of Justice and in his second cabinet in 1926 as Minister of Finance. In 1927, at a convention held in Winnipeg, Bennett was chosen as the leader of the Conservative party and in the general election of 1930 he led his party to victory. He became Prime Minister, taking over at the same time the portfolios of Finance and External Affairs. His period of office coincided with the most severe years of the Great Depression, and his efforts to counter the effects of the economic crisis did not prove successful. His government was voted out of office in Calgary. He was the leader of the opposition until he retired from public life in 1938 and went to live in the south of England. In 1941 he was created Viscount Bennett of Michleham, Calgary and Hopewell. He died at Dorking in 1947. His papers are at the University of New Brunswick.

(See: Ernest, Watkins, R.B. Bennett)

Hilliard Harris William Beyerstein

Social Credit for Camrose 1949-1953

Born at Meeting Creek, Alberta in 1907, he was the son of Fred Beyerstein and Clara Lindquist, his wife, both of whom were of Swedish descent. He was educated at Meeting Creek and Palmer School of Chiropractic, Davenport, Iowa, where he obtained a Doctor of Chiropractic degree. He established his practice in Camrose and was active in the Social Credit movement like several other members of profession. In 1949 he was named the Social Credit candidate for Camrose. He sat in the federal House for one term. In 1953 redistribution eliminated the Camrose riding. He then retired from politics at the age of forty-five. Religion: Lutheran.

Frederick Jack Bigg

Progressive Conservative for Athabasca 1958-1968

Progressive Conservative for Pembina 1968-1972

Born at Meskavaw, Saskatchewan, in 1912, he is the son of Frederick Bigg who was of British descent. He was educated at Prince Albert Collegiate, the University of Saskatchewan and the University of Toronto where he obtained a law degree in 1953. As a young man he joined the Royal Canadian Mounted Police and was a sergeant when he retired from the force. He saw active service with the Royal Canadian Horse Artillery as a captain during the Second World War. He was a lawyer in Westlock when he entered federal politics in 1958 and was elected for the large northern riding of Athabasca. He was re-elected in the 1962, 1963, 1965 and 1968 general elections, the last time for the newly created riding of Pembina. Religion: Anglican.

John Horn Blackmore

Social Credit for Lethbridge 1935-1938

Born at Sublett, Idaho, United States, in 1890, of British descent, he was educated at Cardston and the University of Alberta where he obtained a Bachelor of Arts degree in 1913. He then attended the Calgary normal school. Blackmore married Emily Woolley of Raymond, Alberta, and had large family. He taught at several schools in southern Alberta before becoming the principal at Raymond in 1921, a position he held for the next fourteen years until he entered federal politics. He was the Social Credit candidate for Lethbridge where he defeated the incumbent, General John Stewart. He held the riding for the next twenty-three years. He served at the Social Credit House leader in the Commons from 1935-1944. He was mentioned as a possible successor to the deceased Premier William "Bible Bill" Aberhart in 1943, but the Social Credit caucus passed him over to give the job to Ernest Manning

While in the federal house, he was instrumental in securing federal construction of St. Mary River Dam as well as the Waterton and Belly River dams, the mainstay of Alberta's irrigation project. He was made an honorary Chief of the Kainai tribe of the Kainai Nation Reserve in 1945. His title was motuskumau (Wise Counselor). He is the author of several books on Social Credit theory and was an influential member of the Mormon community.

William John Blair
Conservative for Battle River 1917-1921

Born at Embro, Ontario, in 1875, of Irish descent, he was educated at Woodstock Collegiate Institute and the School of Practical Science, Toronto and obtained a Bachelor of Applied Science. Prior to coming to Alberta, he was a schoolteacher in Ontario and spent seven years as a mining engineer in Cobalt. He then became the mayor of New Liseard, Ontario, 1907-1908. He came west in 1910 where he became a successful farmer in the Provost district of Alberta. He was defeated three times provincially before he ran federally. He was elected in the general election of 1917 as the Unionist member for Battle River. Blair did not stand for re-election in the 1921 election.

Kenneth Alexander Blatchford
Liberal from Edmonton East 1926-1930

Born at Minnedosa, Manitoba, in 1881 of British descent, he was educated at Minnedosa and the Commercial College, Winnipeg. He became an insurance broker and was elected an Edmonton alderman in the early 1920's. He served as mayor of Edmonton from 1924 to 1926. He entered federal politics as a Liberal candidate from Edmonton East in the 1926 general election. He defeated the incumbent, Conservative A.U.W. Bury, by a small majority of 165 votes, but was unseated by Bury four years later. He died in April 1933. Religion: Presbyterian.

Arthur Moren Boutillier
UFA for Vegreville 1925-1926

Born at Halifax, Nova Scotia, in 1869, he was the son of Esrom Boutillier, French, and Anna Spear, his Irish wife. He was educated at the Halifax treasurer of the district of Eagle for many years commencing in 1904. He was active in theU.F.A.movement and entered federal politics in 1925 as the Progressive candidate for the new riding of Vegreville. He was elected with the large majority of 2,460 votes. He did not seek re-election in the next federal election held in 1926. In 1940, he attempted to get re-elected in Vegreville, but failed. Religion: Anglican.

Edwin William "Ted" Brunsden

Progressive Conservative for Medicine Hat 1958-1962

Born in Kent, England, in 1896, he is the son of Samuel Brunsden. He was educated at Calgary, the Olds Agricultural College and the University of Alberta where he obtained a Bachelor of Science degree. He was an agricultural agent in Brooks, Alberta. As a young man he saw active service with the 29th Battalion in the Great War. Entering federal politics in 1957, he was defeated by the Social Crediter Bud Olson at the time. However, in Diefenbaker sweep of Alberta in 1958, he was elected. He was defeated again by Olson in the 1962 federal election, whereupon he retired from active politics. Religion: Anglican.

William Ashbury Buchanan

Liberal for Lethbridge 1911-1921

Summoned to the Senate in 1925.

(See List of Senators)

John Francis Buckley

Liberal for Athabasca, 1930-1931

Born at Butte, Montana, United States, in 1891, he was the son of John Buckley who was of British descent. He came to Canada as a young man in 1911 after being educated in Wales and at the Inner Temple in London, England. He started a law practice in St. Paul, Alberta, before seeing active service with the Princess Patricia's Canadian Light Infantry during the Great War. He entered politics in 1930 when he ran as a Liberal in the large northern riding of Athabasca. He was elected with a 1291 vote majority. He died a year later while still a Member of Parliament. Religion: United Church.

Ambrose Upton Gledstanes Bury

Conservative for Edmonton East 1925-1926

Born at Doronings House, Kildare, Ireland, in 1869, he was the son of Charles Bury, J.P. and Margaret Aylmer, both Anglo-Irish. His mother's family had a long connection with Canada. Matthem, fifth Baron Aylmer, was a Governor-General of Canada during the 1830's and remained in the country. Bury was educated at the Royal School Raphoe, County Donegal, and Trinity College, Dublin University where he received a Master of Arts degree in 1893. He was subsequently called to the Irish Bar as a member of the King's Inns, Dublin, 1906. He then came to Canada and established a law practice in Edmonton. He was called to the Alberta Bar in 1913 and appointed a King's Councilor in 1928. Always interested in politics, Bury was a Conservative candidate in the 1921 provincial election but failed to get elected. The next year he successfully ran for the Edmonton city council. He was an alderman from 1922 to 1925. He was elected as a Conservative in the 1925 federal election, but was defeated by Liberal Blatchford the next year. Bury then became the mayor of Edmonton in 1927 and was re-elected in 1928 and 1929. He returned to federal politics in 1930 when he defeated incumbent Blatchford. He retired from politics in 1935 when he reached the age of 66. Bury was appointed a judge of the Northern District Court in 1936. He died March 1951. Religion: Anglican.

Cora Taylor Casselman

Liberal for Edmonton East 1941-1945

Born at Tara, Ontario, in 1888, she was the daughter of Francis Watt Taylor and Elizabeth Noble, both of British descent. She was educated at Toronto Public School and Queen's University where she obtained a Bachelor of Arts degree. She married Frederick C. Casselman, K.C., an Edmonton lawyer in 1916. Casselman was active in a number of organizations including the University Woman's Club, Council of Social Agencies and the Community Chest. She was elected in 1941 in a by-election caused by the death of her husband. She increased the Liberal majority in a three-way struggle. Her opponents were MacLeod for the Conservatives and Orvis Kennedy, Social Credit, who had held the urban riding from 1938 to 1940. Casselman was then the only woman ever to be elected to represent an Alberta constituency in the federal Parliament. She died in September, 1964.

Frederick Clayton Casselman

Liberal for Edmonton East 1940-1941

Born at Helmsville, Montana, United States in 1885, he was the son of Samual Casselman and Albertina Hillborn, both Canadians. His parents returned to Canada when he was a child of five years. He was educated at Forest and Warford High School, Queen's University (B.A.) and the University of Toronto (LL.B.). Casselman married in 1916 Cora Taylor, daughter of Francis Watt Taylor of Barrie, Ontario. They had one daughter. He saw active service as a sergeant in the Canadian Expeditionary Force in France during the Great War. In 1918 he was commissioned into the Wiltshire regiment. On his return to Canada, he established a legal practice in Edmonton where he became active in civic affairs. He was elected to the Edmonton Public School Board in 1928 and served on it for the next nine years. In 1927 he was elected an alderman and three years later ran against incumbent Socred Orvis Kennedy in Edmonton East. He was successful in his first attempt to enter the federal House. However, he died within that year. His widow, Cora Casselman, ran also as a Liberal in the resulting by-election. She was victorious and was then the only woman Alberta had ever sent to Ottawa as a Member of Parliament.

Douglas Marmaduke Caston

Progressive Conservative for Jasper-Edson 1967-1968

Born at Macklin, Saskatchewan, in 1917, he is the son of John E. Caston and Edna Walker, both Canadians of British descent. He was educated at the Macklin newspaper and was president of the Yellowhead Press. He saw active service in the Second World War in Europe in the Canadian Air Force. Caston was first elected to the Commons in a by-election caused when Dr. Hugh Horner resigned his federal seat in order to run provincially in 1967. His majority was 2,861 votes. The Riding of Jasper-Edson disappeared in the redistribution prior to the 1968 federal election. Caston failed to obtain the official Progressive Conservative nomination in the new-created riding of Rocky Mountain. However, he ran as an Independent Conservative, splitting the anti-government vote which enabled Liberal Allen Sulatycky to take the seat. Caston ran third in a six-way contest. He died June 26, 1996 at the age of 78. Religion: Anglican.

Percy Griffith Davies

Conservative for Athabasca 1932-1935

Born at Edmonton in 1902, he was the son of Arthur Davies and Mary Parry, both of British descent. His father was mayor of Strathcona for several years. He was educated at Strathcona High School and the University of Alberta where he obtained a Bachelor of Arts and a Law degree. While at the University he became the secretary-treasurer of the national federation of Canadian university students and the president of the students' union. He was established a law practice at Clyde, Alberta, and entered federal politics as a Conservative in 1932 in a by-election caused by the death of Liberal John Buckley, MP for Athabasca. He had a narrow victory margin of 324 votes. He was under thirty years of age when he was first elected to the Commons. He was not a candidate three years later when Alberta shifted towards the Social Credit Party. He died in 1900 at the age of 87. Religion: United Church.

Donald Watson Davis

Conservative for Alberta, N.W.T. 1887-1896

Born November 3, 1849 in Windham County, on a farm near Londonderry, Vermont, U.S.A., of Anglo-Irish descent. The state census of 1860 lists him as a "farm labourer" at the age of 11. In 1865 he enlisted in the Union army and he saw active service during the final months of the American Civil War. Two years later he enlisted in the American Army where he served as an active quartermaster sergeant with he 13th United States Infantry at Fort Show, Montana Territories. In 1879 he took part in a raid on a Peigan encampment. In 1871 he was demobilized and became an agent for the I.G. Baker Company. By 1873 he was with J.J. Healy as a whisky trader working out of Fort Whoop-Up (or Fort Hamilton) on the Oldman River near the site of the present city of Lethbridge. Davis moved to Fort Macleod where he worked as a carpenter. Later he again became an agent for the I.G. Baker Company and managed the firm's Fort Macleod store. Taciturn and close-mouthed concerning his army life and his dealing as a whisky trader, he became a prominent citizen. His reformation was completed when he became an agent for the I.G. Baker Company and adopted the Anglican faith. In December 1886 he applied to become a British subject; his papers were signed by James F. Macleod, Magistrate (q.v.). In 1887 he married Lily Elizabeth Josephine Grier, a Fort

Macleod schoolteacher and sister of David Johnston Grier, a former member of the Northwest Mounted Police who became Mayor of Fort Macleod and was a wealthy rancher in the area. It was on his honeymoon that he filed the nomination papers for his candidacy as the first Member of Parliament to be returned from the District of Alberta, Northwest Territories.

Davis was returned as the Conservative member for the new Alberta riding in 1888. He sat in the House of Commons for nine years until he vacated his seat on being appointed chief federal customs officer for the remote Yukon Territory in 1896. Upon his arrival at Fort Cudahay, the Northwest Mounted Police post, he met John J. Healy for whom he had worked in the old isolated place in the "out-back". However, civilization had followed from a remote outpost to a city of 20,000 miners and gold seekers in a matter of months. The collector of customs was the most prominent government official in residence at the boomtown. On June 2, 1902 he resigned from the civil service and became a gold miner. He died on June 6 1906 at Dawson City; his funeral service was held at St. Paul's Anglican Church.

Frederick Davis

Conservative for Calgary East 1925-1926

Born at Mitchell, Ontario, in 1868, he was the son of W.R. Davis, who was of British descent. His father was editor and proprietor of a weekly newspaper, The Mitchell Advocate, for some fifty-eight years. Davis was elected councilor, reeve and mayor of his hometown before he came to Alberta. He ran provincially in the 1917 general election as an Independent Conservative for the Gleichen constituency. He was the winner in a three-way contest and sat in the Legislature for the next four years. He entered federal politics in 1925 and was elected in Calgary East. He was not able to hold the seat in the next general election half a year later. Religion: Anglican.

John Decore

Liberal for Vegreville 1949-1957

Born at Andrew, Alberta, in 1909, of Ukrainian descent, he was educated at Andrew, Edmonton, and at the University of Alberta where he obtained a B.A. and L.L.G. While he was qualifying himself as a lawyer, he taught in the Vegreville High School. He established his law practice in Edmonton and Vegreville. He entered federal politics in 1949 when he stood for the Vegreville riding. He won the seat and was re-elected four years later. He did not stand in 1957. Decore was named a Q.C. in 1964. He became a judge of the District Court of northern Alberta. He died on November 11, 1994 at the age of 85. Religion: Orthodox.

James McCrie Douglas

Liberal for Strathcona, 1909-1921

Born at Middleville, Ontario, in 1867, he was the son of Rev James Douglas, of British descent. He received his education at Morris, Manitoba. As a young man he came west to Edmonton in 1894 and then to Strathcona, where he established himself as a merchant in 1901. He was a member of the Strathcona city council for two years. Entering federal politics in 1909, he ran as the Liberal candidate in a by-election caused by the death of the sitting member, Dr. Wilbert McIntrye, and was elected by acclamation. He held the constituency for the next twelve years. Douglas was defeated in 1921 when he ran as a Conservative candidate. He went on to serve as the Mayor of Edmonton from 1929 to 1931. He died March 16, 1950 at the age of 83. Religion: Presbyterian.

Cliff Downey

Progressive Conservative for Battle River 1968-1972

First elected to the House of Commons in the 1968 general election, he had one of the largest majorities in Canada totaling 11,603 votes. Tory farmer Cliff Smallwood had previously half the constituency since the Diefenbaker sweep of 1958. In April 1972, Harry M. Kuntz, a forty-three-year-old Camrose alderman, won the Progressive Conservative nomination for the forthcoming election.

Manley Justin Edwards

Liberal for Calgary West 1940-1945

Born at Caistorville, Ontario, in 1892, he was educated at Hamilton, Ontario, Calgary normal school, and the University of Alberta (L.L.B.).

He taught in Alberta schools while getting his law degree. He established his law practice in Calgary and was active for years in service clubs. He was a national president of Kinsmen Clubs of Canada. He was a Calgary alderman from 1929 to 1950. Edwards ran against incumbent Conservative D.G.L. Cunnington in Calgary West in the 1940 election. He was successful in capturing R.B. Bennett's old seat. He only spent one term in the Federal House. He was appointed a judge of the southern Alberta District Court in 1950. Edwards died while still a judge in May, 1962 at Calgary. Religion: United Church.

Robert Fair

Social Credit for Battle River 1935-1954

Born at Keelognes, Ireland in 1891, he was educated there before he came to Canada in 1914. Fair married in 1919 the daughter of C.S. Holmstrom of Paradise Valley, Alberta. He was a farmer in the Paradise Valley district. First elected to the Commons as a Social Crediter in 1935 for the rural riding of Battle River, he held the seat until his death some twenty years later in November 1954. Religion: United Church.

Frank John William Fane

Progressive Conservative for Vegreville 1958-1968

Born at Beaver Lake, Alberta, 1897, he is the son of Frank W. Fane and Margaret Duff, both of British descent. His father had been an unsuccessful Conservative candidate for the Victoria constituency in 1905 and 1909. He was educated at Beaver Lake, Vegreville, Camrose normal school and the University of Alberta. He taught briefly as a young man before seeing active service with the Canadian Expeditionary Force during the Great War. On his return from overseas he became a farmer in the Mundare district. He was active for many years in municipal affairs, serving both on the municipal board and the school board. He was an unsuccessful Conservative candidate for the Vegreville riding in the 1940 and again in 1957. He was first elected at the age of sixty-one in 1958 when all seventeen Alberta ridings went Conservative. He was re-elected in 1962, 1963 and 1965. He retired in 1968. Religion: Anglican.

Robert Gardiner

UFA for Medicine Hat 1921-1925

Born in Aberdeenshire, Scotland, in 1879, he came to Canada in 1902 after being educated in Scotland. Councilor and Reeve of the municipal district of Golden Centre, Alberta from 1914 to 1921, he was first elected to the Common in a by-election caused by the death of Arthur Sifton in 1921. He was re-elected in 1925, 1926, and 1930, but was defeated in 1935. Gardiner had been elected theU.F.A.president in 1931 when Henry Wise Wood had retired. He died in February 1945, at Calgary. Gardiner never married. Religion: Presbyterian.

Edward Joseph Garland

UFA for Bow River 1921-1935

Born at Dublin, Ireland, in 1885, he came to Canada in 1909. He was educated at Belvidera College and Trinity College, Dublin University. He left before he obtained a degree. He became a farmer in the Ramsey district of central Alberta. He became active in the United Farmers of Alberta movement, being an executive officer of the farm organization in 1921. He represented Bow River riding in Ottawa from 1921 to 1935. Social Credit member Charles Johnston defeated him in 1935. Religion: Roman Catholic.

Dr. Frederick Gershaw

Liberal for Medicine Hat 1925-1935 and 1940-1945

Senator from Alberta 1945-1963

(See: List of Senators)

General William Antrobus

Conservative for Edmonton West 1917-1921

Senator from Alberta 1921-1944

(See: List of Senators)

Deane Roscoe Gundlock

Progressive Conservative for Lethbridge 1948-1972

Born at Warner, Alberta, in 1914, he is the son of Emil Herman Gundlock, British, and Arline Huilt, American. He was educated at West Denver. He was a successful farmer and partner in an import-export company. He served on the local school board (1946-1948) before entering federal politics in 1948. He was elected for Lethbridge and held the seat in the next four general elections. In January 1972, he retired from politics. He died September 10, 1986 at the age of 72. Religion: Protestant.

Dr. William Samuel Hall

Social Credit for Edmonton East 1935-1938

Born at Mount Forrests, Ontario, in 1871, he was the son of William Hall and Mary Gillies, both Canadians. He was educated at Hawkesbury, Ontario, and Royal College of Dental Surgeons and the University of Toronto where he obtained L.D.S. and D.D.S. degrees. He came to Edmonton to establish his dental practice. Dr. Hall was an admirer of William Aberhart and ran as a Social Credit candidate in the 1935 provincial election. He was defeated at the polls, but obtained the Socred nomination for Edmonton East riding and was elected to the Commons in the federal election held later that year. He was sixty-six years or age at the time. He died two years later while still a sitting Member of Parliament. Orvis Kennedy held the seat for the Social Credit in the resulting by-election. Religion: Baptist.

Howard Hadden Halladay

Unionist of Bow River 1917-1921

Born at Elgin, Ontario, in 1878, he was educated at Athens, Ontario, and Winnipeg. He came west and became an insurance agent and farmer. He was mayor of Hanna, Alberta, from 1913 to 1918. He was first elected to the Commons as a Unionist in the 1917 general election. He was not a candidate in the 1921 federal election. Religion: Methodist.

R.F.L. "Dick" Hanna

Liberal for Edmonton Strathcona 1953-1957

Born at Monaghan, Ireland, in 1913, he was educated at Mountjoy School, Dublin, Drumheller, Calgary normal school and the University of Alberta where he obtained a Bachelor of Arts degree. He taught in Alberta during the 1930's before seeing active service in the RCAF during the Second World War. He worked for the Veterans Land Act administration after leaving the armed services. He entered civic politics in 1948 when he was elected as an Edmonton alderman. He was on the city council for five years. In the 1953 general election he ran as a Liberal candidate in an urban riding. He won the seat by 151 votes. His nearest rival was Orvis Kennedy, president of the Social Credit League and a former Member of Parliament. He failed in his re-election bid, being defeated by Syd Thompson. He went on to become an insurance salesman. Religion: United Church.

Rev. Ernest George Hansell

Social Credit for Macleod 1935-1958

Born at Norwich, England, in 1895, he came to Canada at the age of nine. Educated at the Bible Institute of Los Angeles and the Southern Divinity School, Dallas, Texas. He became a minister of the Christian Church in Vulcan and was a special lecturer at the Alberta Bible College. He entered politics in 1935 and represented the southern Alberta riding of Macleod in Ottawa for the next twenty-three years. He was defeated in 1958 by Progressive Conservative Dr. Kindt. Hansell then entered provincial politics and was the Member of the Legislature for Okotoks-High River from 1959 to 1963. He retired at sixty-eight years of age. Hansell died in December 1965, at Calgary.

Douglas Harkness

Progressive Conservative for Calgary North 1945-1968

Progressive Conservative for Calgary Centre 1968-1972

Minister of Northern Affairs 1957-1958

Minister of Agriculture 1957-1960

Minister of National Defense 1960-1963

Born at Toronto in 1903, he was the son of William Harkness and Janet Scott, both of British descent. He was educated at Calgary Central Collegiate and the University of Alberta where he obtained a Bachelor's degree. He first became a high school teacher and later a farmer. During the Second World War, Harkness saw active service in Sicily, Italy, and northwest Europe as an artillery officer. He was first elected to the House of Commons in 1956 and was re-elected a total of eight times as one of the Members for the city of Calgary. Harkness was named to Diefenbaker's first cabinet in 1957 as Minister of Northern Affairs and National Resources. A few weeks later he was appointed Minister of Agriculture, a post he held for the next three years. In 1960 the fifty-seven-year-old former artillery colonel was transferred to the Department of National Defense. He was the Minister of Defense until early 1963 when he quit the federal cabinet due to a policy disagreement with Diefenbaker. He died May 2, 1999 at the age of 96. Religion: Presbyterian.

Dr. Hu Harries

Liberal for Edmonton Strathcona 1968-1972

Born at Strathmore, Alberta, 1921, of British descent, he was educated at the University of Alberta, University of Toronto, and Iowa State University (Ph.D. degree). He served from 1953 to 1959 as an Edmonton alderman. He was on the faculty of the University of Alberta when he was first elected to the House of Commons in 1968. He referred to himself as an economist. He died August 26, 1986. Religion: United Church.

William Hayhurst

Social Credit for Vegreville 1935-1940

Born at Lyvennet Mill, Morland, England in 1887, he was the son of Gilbert Hayhurst and Sara Burrow, both British. He was educated at Morland and Appleby grammar school before coming to Canada in 1910. He later attended the University of Alberta. Hayhurst was for years the principal of the Vegreville High School. He was also the reeve of Minburn from 1923-1924. He first ran federally in 1930 but was defeated. In 1935 he tried again, this time as a Social Crediter, and was successful. He retired from politics after only serving one term in the federal House. Religion: United Church.

Anthony Hlynka
Social Credit for Vegreville 1940-1949

Born in Western Ukraine in 1907, he came to Canada with his parents when he was still a child. He was educated in Delph and Edmonton and attended the technical school in Edmonton. He worked as a journalist and was a publisher of a weekly newspaper. He entered federal politics in 1940 and won the Vegreville riding for the Social Credit movement. He was re-elected five years later but failed to hold the seat in 1949 when he was opposed by Liberal lawyer John Decore. He died in 1957 at the age of 49. Religion: Greek Orthodox.

Ambrose Holowach
Social Credit for Edmonton East 1953-1958

Born at Edmonton in 1914, he was the son of Sam Holowach and Jossephine Dwornik, both Ukrainians. He was educated at Edmonton and studied music in Europe, supporting himself by writing on music festivals. During the Second World War he served with the Canadian signal corps. He owned and operated the family dry-cleaning firm. He failed in 1949 in his first bid to get into Parliament but was successful four years later in the urban riding of Edmonton East. He lost his seat in the Diefenbaker landslide of 1958. However, the next year he entered provincial politics. He represented an Edmonton constituency in the Legislature for the next twelve years until the Lougheed sweeper of 1971 unseated him. In 1962 he was appointed Provincial Secretary and was the chairman of the Alberta Centennial Committee in 1967. He was defeated in the 1975 provincial election by Dave King and retired from politics. Religion: Ukrainian Catholic.

Dr. Hugh MacArthur Horner
Progressive Conservative for the Jasper-Edson 1958-1965

Born at Blaine Lake, Saskatchewan, in 1925, he was the son of the late Senator Ralph Horner and brother to Jack Horner, Conservative M.P. for Crowfoot. He was educated at Blaine Lake, University of Western Ontario (M.D.). Upone obtaining his medical degree, he established a practice at Barrhead, Alberta. He was first elected to the Commons in 1958 election for the Jasper-Edson riding. He resigned his seat in 1965 in order to enter provincial politics. He was one of the small group of Conservatives elected to the Legislature in 1967. He was re-elected in 1971 and was named to Lougheed's cabinet as Deputy Premier and Minister of Agriculture. He died March 25, 1997 at the age of 72. Religion: United Church.

John Henry "Jack" Horner

Progressive Conservative for Acadia 1958-1968

Born at Blain Lake, Saskatchewan, in 1927, he was the son of Senator Ralph Horner and younger brother of Dr. Hugh Horner, Deputy Premier of Alberta and Minister of Agriculture in the Lougheed cabinet. He was educated at the University of Alberta and was a successful rancher in the Pollockville district of Alberta. He entered federal politics in 1958 when he was elected the Tory Member of Parliament for Acadia. This riding disappeared in the 1968 redistribution, but Horner was elected for the new-created riding of Crowfoot. He was one of the most colourful Members in the federal House. He died on November 18, 2004. Religion: United Church.

William Irvine

Labour for Calgary East 1921-1925

UFA for Wetaskiwin 1926-1935

Born in the Shetland Islands, Scotland, in 1885, he came to Canada as a youth in 1902. He was educated at Manitoba and Wesley Colleges, Winnipeg. Irvine was a Presbyterian Minister at Emo, Ontario 1913-1915, and a Unitarian clergyman at Calgary 1915-1919. He was acquitted in ecclesiastical courts of the charge of heresy in 1914. The author of several pamphlets, he was editor of the Western Farmer and The People's Weekly. After the Great War he homesteaded in the Bentley district. He became a successful farmer. He was active in politics all his life, running unsuccessfully both provincially and federally in 1917. He was first elected to Parliament as aLabourcandidate in Calgary East in 1921. He failed to hold the seat in the 1925 general election, but was successful in Wetaskiwin as aU.F.A.candidate the next year, which he represented in Ottawa for nine years. Irvine was active in the CCF party for many years. He was elected for the federal riding of Cariboo in 1945 but was defeated again four years later. Irvine died in October 1962, at Edmonton. Religion: Unitarian.

Norman Jaques

Social Credit for Wetaskiwin 1935-1949

Born at London, England, 1880, he was educated at Eastbourne College prior to coming to Canada as a young man in 1901. Jaques homesteaded in the Mirror district of Alberta, becoming a successful farmer. He entered federal politics in 1935, winning the rural riding of Wetaskiwin. He represented this constituency for the next fourteen years in Ottawa. He died while still a Member in January 1949. Religion: Anglican.

Lincoln Henry Jelliff

Progressive for Lethbridge 1921-1930

Born at Oneida, Illinois, United States, in 1865, he was the son of Fletcher Jelliff, whose ancestors came to America from Britain in colonial days. He was educated at Oneida and Know College, Galesburg, where he obtained an M.A. He came to Canada in 1902 to homestead in the Raley district. Jelliff was a successful farmer. He successfully ran for the House of Common in 1921 as a Progressive. He was re-elected in 1926 but was defeated by Tory General John Stewart in the 1930 federal election. He died on September 24, 1962 at the age of 97. Religion: Congregationalist.

Charles Edward Johnston

Social Credit for Bow River 1935-1958

Born at May Mills, Michigan, in 1899, he was the son of Alfred Johnston, a Canadian, and Mary Burgett, his American wife. Coming to Canada while still a child in 1906, he was educated at the University of Alberta, then became a school teacher in the Three Hills district. He was first elected to Parliament in 1935 as a Social Crediter. He was re-elected five times before being defeated by Conservative Eldon Woolliams in 1958. Johnston then entered provincial politics and sat for two terms as the Social Credit member for Calgary-Bowness. He retired from politics in 1967 at the age of 68. Johnston died in December, 1971, while on holiday in Houston, Texas. Religion: United Church.

Donald Ferdinand Killner

Progressive for Edmonton East 1921-1925

UFA for Athabasca 1926-1930

Born in 1879 at Ethel, Ontario, he was the son of Joseph Kellner, Canadian, and Catherine Forsyth, his Scottish wife. He was educated at the public schools and at Listowel High School before becoming a farmer. He was first elected to Parliament for Edmonton East in 1921. He was defeated in 1925 in his first attempt to represent the large northern rural riding of Athabasca. However, Killner was successful in the federal election half a year later, running this time as a U.F.A. candidate. He died April 1935, in Edmonton. Religion: Presbyterian.

Donald Macbeth Kennedy

UFA for Edmonton West 1921-1925

UFA for Peace River 1925-1935

Born at Ballinlaig, Perthshire Scotland, in 1884, he came to Canada as a young man in 1903. He was educated in Scotland and at Brandon College, Manitoba. He homesteaded in the Waterhole district of Alberta, and in time became a successful farmer. He became active in local politics, serving as a municipal councilor, and in the United Farmers of Alberta organization. Kennedy was elected for the provincial riding of Peace River in 1921, but resigned to enter federal politics. He ran in Edmonton West in the 1921 federal election and won. Four years later he changed constituencies and was successful in his bid to be the Peace River representative in Parliament. He was re-elected in 1926 and again in 1930 but failed to hold the riding against his Social Credit opponent in 1935. He died on September 25, 1957 at the age of 73. Religion: Baptist.

Orvis Alexander Kennedy

Social Credit for Edmonton East 1938-1940

Born at Dryden, Ontario, in 1907, he was of British descent. He was educated there and at Lafine, Alberta. He was a hardware salesman in Edmonton. He became active in politics as a Social Crediter and was an early supporter of William Aberhard, whom he knew through his association with the Prophetic Bible Institute. He was a provincial candidate in the 1935 election for the multi-member Edmonton constituency. After the first count he was the sixth in a field of twenty-seven candidates for the six-member constituency. However he failed to hold his position in the re-counts, being narrowly defeated. Three years later, upon the death of Dr. Hall, Social Credit Member of Parliament for Edmonton East, he entered federal politics. He had been Hall's official agent in 1935. It was the first by-election in the province since the Social Credit sweeper three years before. He won the three-way struggle, defeating Conservative Walter Cleverey and Liberal Robert Marshall. The night of the by-election Premier Aberhart danced an "Irish jig" when it was clear that the Social Credit party had held the riding. Kennedy failed in his re-election bid in 1940 and Conservative lawyer Frederick Casselman captured the seat. He then became the president of the Social Credit League and chief party organizer. For the next thirty years he was the organizer of victory for Premier Manning in seven provincial general elections.

Dr. Lawrence Elliott Kindt

Progressive Conservative for Macleod 1958-1968

Born at Kiona, State of Washington in 1901, his father homesteaded in the Nanton district in 1904. He was educated at Nanton and the University of Alberta (B.Sc. 1927), University of Minnesota (M.A. 1930), and the American University, Washington D.C. (Ph.D. 1940). He was a director in his own economic consulting firm in Calgary as well as a federal agricultural economist. He entered federal politics as a Conservative in 1958 and was elected for the rural riding of Macleod. Kindt held the constituency until he retired, undefeated, in 1968. Religion: United Church.

John Charles Landeryou

Social Credit for Calgary East 1935-1940

Born at Harriston, Ontario, in 1905, he was of British descent. He was educated at Calgary and the Business College, St. Louis, Missouri, before becoming a chef in Calgary. He entered federal politics as a Social Crediter in the 1935 general election and won the Calgary East constituency. He was defeated in his bid to hold the seat five years later by a narrow 485 vote margin. The victor in this election was G.H. Ross, who later became a Senator. Landeryou then moved to Lethbridge where he was an insurance agent. He entered provincial politics in the 1944 general election and became Lethbridge's representative in the Legislature. During the twenty-seven years he was an MLA Landeryou took a backseat. Both he and R.S. Lee, MLA for Taber, were expelled from the Social Credit movement in 1955 as a result of a scandal. However, both were re-elected with increased majorities in the general election later that year, and were re-admitted into the party. He retired from politics in 1971 at the age of sixty-six. His party, however, was able to elect two Social Crediters in the 1971 provincial election that saw the defeated of the Social Credit administration after being in office thirty-six years. Religion: Baptist.

Solon Earl Low
Social Credit for Peace River 1945-1958

National Leader of the Social Credit Movement 1945-1958, he was born at Cardston, Alberta, in 1900. He was the son of James Low (Scotch), a university-educated businessman and a member of the constitutional convention of the State of Utah in the 1880's. Low was educated at Cardston, Calgary normal school, University of Alberta, and University of South California. He was a well-known high school principal at Stirling when he entered provincial politics in 1935 as a Social Crediter. He was elected for the riding of Warner and was named to Aberhart's cabinet as the Provincial Treasurer in 1937. He was defeated in the 1940 general election, but he was returned by acclamation in Vegreville the same year when the sitting member, George Woytkiw, resigned. His name was mentioned as a possible successor to William Aberhart when he died in 1943. Low remained the Provincial Treasurer until 1944. He was also the Minister of Education from 1943 to 1944. He resigned his seat in the Legislature in 1945 to enter federal politics after being named the national leader of the Social Credit movement. He represented the large Peace River constituency in Ottawa for the next thirteen years before becoming a victim of the Diefenbaker sweep in 1958. Low, after twenty-three years of active politics, returned to the classroom in his old school in southern Alberta. Later, he was named a magistrate by Premier Manning. He died in 1961. Religion: Mormon.

William Thomas Lucas

UFA for Camrose 1925-1930

Born at Baileboro, Ontario, in 1875, he was of British descent. Educated at Baileboro and at the Ontario Agricultural College, Guelph, he was a farmer in the Lougheed district of Alberta. He became active in the United Farmers of Alberta movement and ran as a Progressive in the constituency of Victoria in 1921 and was elected by a more than 9,600 vote majority. Four years later Lucas was successful in his re-election bid in the newly created riding of Camrose which he held for the next ten years as a U.F.A. member. Religion: Anglican.

Marcel Lambert

Progressive Conservative for Edmonton West 1957-1984

Speaker of the House of Commons 1962-1963

Minister of Veteran Affairs 1963

Born at Edmonton in 1919, he was the son of J.E. Lambert, a Canadian and Marie Kiwit, who was Belgian. His grandfather, L.J.A. Lambert, represented that constituency of St. Alberta in the Northwest Territories Legislature in Regina from 1901 to 1905. He was educated at the University of Alberta and was named a Rhodes scholar, which permitted him to obtain a law degree from Oxford. As a young man he briefly worked in a bank in Morinville, Alberta, before joining the Canadian army during the Second World War. He took part in the ill-fated Dieppe raid in the summer of 1943 and was taken prisoner by the Germans and spent the remainder of the war in a prisoner of war camp. Upon his return to Canada Lambert attended the University of Alberta where he obtained a Bachelor of Commerce degree in 1947. He was named a Rhodes Emery Jamieson of Edmonton; he was called to the Alberta Bar in 1951. Interested in politics, he attempted to be elected to the Legislature in 1952 for the multi-member Edmonton constituency but was defeated. He was, however, successful in his first bid to get into the Commons in the 1957 general election. In the 1958 election he had a 22,393 vote majority over his nearest rival, Liberal Henry Dyde, who was also a Rhodes scholar. In 1962 Lambert was a Speaker of the House of Commons, and for a few weeks in the spring of 1963 he was in Diefenbaker's cabinet as Minister of Veteran Affairs. He died September 24, 2000. Religion: Roman Catholic.

Michael Luchkovich

UFA for Vegreville 1926-1930

Born in 1892 at Shamokin, Pennsylvania, United States, he was of Ukrainian descent. He came to Canada as a youth in 1907 and attended the University of Manitoba where he received a Bachelor of Arts degree. He then became a teacher at Vegreville. Luchkovich entered federal politics to run as aU.F.A.candidate in the constituency of Vegreville that he won with a narrow majority. He died April 21, 1973. Religion: Greek Catholic.

(See: Michael Luchkovich, A Ukrainian Canadian in Parliament (1965)

Albert Frederick MacDonald

Liberal for Edmonton East 1949-1953

Born at Winnipeg in 1901, he was the son of Alberta MacDonald and Margaret Veitch, both of British descent. He was educated at Winnipeg's Wesley College. He was a Canadian National Railway employee and active in the trade union movement. He had seen active service with the Edmonton fusiliers during the Second World War. In 1949 he entered federal politics when he ran as the Liberal candidate in Edmonton East. He was elected and served for one term in the Commons. He failed in his re-election bid in 1953, being defeated by Social Crediter Ambrose Holowach. He died August 20, 1976. Religion: Presbyterian.

Henry Arthur Mackie

Unionist for Edmonton East 1917-1921

Born at Cookshire, Quebec, in 1878, he was the son of Joseph Ignatius Mackie and Clothilde Lantangue. He was educated at Bishop's University (B.A.) and McGill University before coming to western Canada where he established a law practice in Edmonton. He was named a K.C. in 1921. Mackie entered federal politics as a Unionist in 1917 and won the urban riding of Edmonton East. He was defeated in the 1921 election. He died in November 1945, at Edmonton.

James Angus MacKinnon

Liberal for Edmonton West 1935-1949

Minister without Portfolio 1939-1940

Minister of Trade and Commerce 1940-1948

Minister of Fisheries 1949

Minister of Mines and Resources 1949

Summoned to the Senate 1949

Minister without Portfolio 1949-1950

(See: List of Senators)

Charles Alexander Magrath

Conservative for Medicine Hat 1908-1911

Born at North Augusta, Upper Canada, in 1860, he was of British descent. Educated privately, he came west to the Northwest Territories as a young man. He worked there as a land surveyor and irrigation engineer until 1885, when he joined the Galt interests in various enterprises. He was the first mayor of the town of Lethbridge. He sat for Lethbridge in the Regina Parliament from 1891 to 1902, serving as Minister Without Portfolio in the Haultin cabinet, 1898-1901. Entering federal politics as a Conservative, he represented Medicine Hat in the Commons from 1908 to 1911. Magrath was defeated in 1911 by the young publisher of The Lethbridge Herald, WA. Buchanan. In the years that followed he acted on many boards and advisory committees. Magrath was the author of Canada's Growth and Some Problems Affecting It (1910) and of historical articles on the Canadian West. Magrath married for the first time in 1887 Margaret Holmes Mair, who was the daughter of Charles Mair of the patriotic "Canada's First" movement and author of Tecumseh a Drama. They had one son. He married for a second time in 1899 to Mabel Lilias, daughter of Sir Alexander T. Galt, one of the Fathers of Confederation, and brother of Elliot T. Galt who became a pioneer in railway and irrigation projects in southern Alberta. They had two daughters. He died October, 1949, at Victoria at the age of eighty-nine years.

Terrence James Nugent

Progressive Conservative for Edmonton Strathcona 1958-1968

Born at Taber, Alberta, in 1920, he was the son of Patrick Nugent and Bridget Duke, both Canadian of British descent. He was educated at Camrose, Edmonton, and the University of Alberta where he obtained a B.A. and an L.L.B. degree. He served in the Canadian Air Force during the Second World War before he established his law practice in Edmonton. He was an unsuccessful Tory candidate in the 1957 federal election but won the Edmonton Strathcona riding in the 1958 election. He had a colourful career in the House of Commons. He represented Edmonton Strathcona in Ottawa for ten years before being defeated by Liberal Dr. Hu Harris in the 1968 general election. Nugent then turned to civic politics and was elected an Edmonton alderman. He served for one term.

Frank Oliver

Independent for Alberta 1896

Liberal for Alberta and then Edmonton 1900-1917

Minister of the Interior 1905-1911

Born in Chinguacousy, Ontario, in 1853 he was the son of Allan Bowsfield. His mother's maiden name was Oliver, which he adopted as his own. He worked on a number of newspapers in Ontario before moving to the Northwest Territories in the 1870's. In 1876 he began freighting by cart into Edmonton, which was only a village at the time. In 1880 Oliver founded Alberta's first newspaper, The Edmonton Bulletin, over which he retained control until 1923. He was always interested in politics; and became a member of the North West Council in 1883. He was elected to the Legislative Assembly, which succeeded the Council, with wider powers, 1888 to 1896. He was the Member of Parliament for some twenty years, commencing in 1896. Upon the resignation of Clifford Sifton in 1905, Oliver joined the Laurier cabinet as Minister of the Interior and Superintendent of Indian Affairs. He remained the federal cabinet minister for Alberta until the defeat of the government in 1911, and did much to encourage immigration onto the western prairies. He was one of the few prominent western Liberals to support Laurier in the 1917 general election. He led General Griesbach in the civil vote, but failed to obtain a majority of the service votes cast. He then retired from active politics at the age of sixty-four. He was appointed a member of the Board of Railway Commissioners in 1923 and served for five years. When Alberta was created a province in 1905, there was a strong possibility that Oliver would become the first Premier. However he was more interested in obtaining a federal cabinet appointment, which he obtained that year. He died March 1933, at Ottawa.

Horace Andrew "Bud" Olson

Social Credit for Medicine Hat 1957- 1958

Liberal for Medicine Hat- 1968-1972

Minister of Agriculture 1968-1972

Born at Iddesleigh, Alberta, in 1925, he was of Norwegian descent. His parents were born in North Dakota and came to Canada in 1912. He was educated at Iddesleigh and Medicine Hat. He was a farmer and merchant, and had a large farm in the Rainy Hills district of Alberta. He entered federal politics as a Social Crediter and won the Medicine Hat riding in 1957. Ted Brunsden defeated him in the Diefenbaker landslide in March, 1958. However, he captured the seat again for the Social Credit in 1962 and sat with Robert Thompson, Social Credit National Leader until the spring of 1968 when he crossed the floor of the House to join the Liberals. He ran in the general election of that year as a Liberal and held the seat. He was named to the Trudeau cabinet in 1968 as the Minister of Agriculture. He was actively interested in Western Canadian history. He died February 14, 2002 at the age of 76. Religion: Lutheran.

Patrick Morgan Mahoney

Liberal for Calgary South 1968-1972

Born at Winnipeg in 1929, he was educated at Calgary and the University of Alberta (B.A. and an L.L.B. degree). A corporation executive, he has been active in promoting professional football. He was president of the Canadian Football League and also president of the Stampede Football club. He was first elected to the federal Parliament for Calgary South in the 1968 general election by defeating Ray Ballard, the incumbent Conservative member. His majority was under eight hundred in a three-way contest that saw close to 23,000 votes cast. On January 28, 1972, Mahoney was appointed by Prime

Minister Trudeau, Minister of State with special responsibility for continuing review of tax policy. He died June 8, 2012 at the age of 83.

James Alexander Marshall
Social Credit for Camrose 1935-1949

Born at Lurgan, Ireland, in 1888, he was educated there and at the Kildare Training College for Teachers in Dublin. He came to Canada in 1912 to become a teacher in the Bashaw district of Alberta. He married Edna Lawrence of Iowa, United States, in 1915. His only daughter, Margaret Maureen, married Randolph McKinnon, an Edmonton schoolteacher, who was a Social Credit Minister of Education in the 1960's. Marshall was the municipal secretary and entered federal politics in 1935 when he was elected for the Camrose constituency. He represented the riding in Ottawa for the next fourteen years. He was not a candidate in 1949. Religion: Anglican.

Donald Frank Mazankowski
Progressive Conservative for Vegreville 1968-1993

Born at Viking, Alberta, in 1935, he is of Polish descent. Educated at Viking, he is a successful Vegreville businessman. He was a trustee on the Vegreville separate school board from 1963 to 1968. He entered federal politics in the 1968 general election. His majority was 10,789 votes. He would go on to serve as Minister for the Crown and was responsible for several portfolios. Prime Minister Brian Mulroney appointed him Deputy Prime Minister in 1986. He received the Order of Canada in 2000. Religion: Catholic.

Maitland Stewart McCarthy
Conservative for Calgary 1904-1911

Born at Orangeville, Ontario, he was the son of Judge McCarthy and his wife, Jennie Frances Stewart, both Irish. He was educated at Port Hope, Ontario, and Trinity University, Toronto (B.A. degree). He established his law practice and entered federal politics in 1904 when he stood as the Conservative candidate for the Calgary seat in the Commons. He was successful and represented Calgary in Ottawa for the next seven years. In 1908 the provincial leadership of the

Conservative party was offered to him. McCarthy refused it on the ground that to resign his seat would compromise his honor, for his election had been protested and, until the case was decided, resignation would look like an admission of guilt. He was not a candidate in 1911. He was named a judge in 1914. He died May 1930, at Montreal. Religion: Anglican.

Dr. Wilbert McIntyre
Liberal for Strathcona 1905-1909

Born at Rosedale, Ontario, in 1867, he was of British descent. He was educated at Owen Sound Collegiate Institute and the University of Toronto where he obtained a Bachelor of Medicine. He came west as a young man and started to practice at Strathcona. He was a successful physician. Dr. McIntyre became the president of the Strathcona Board of Trade in 1904. He entered federal politics as the Liberal candidate for Strathcona in the by-election caused when Peter Talbot was appointed to the Senate in 1905. He defeated his only opponent, Dr. Crang. He died while a sitting Member of Parliament in 1909. Religion: Presbyterian.

Archibald Hugh Mitchell
Social Credit for Medicine Hat 1935-1945

Born at Macleod, Alberta, in 1903, he was the son of Archibald Mitchell who was of British descent. He was educated at Claresholm Agricultural College and the University of Alberta. Mitchell was a farmer in the Medicine Hat district. He entered federal politics in 1935 when he ran as a Social Credit candidate for Medicine Hat. In this election he defeated incumbent Liberal Dr. Gershaw. However, five years later, Gershaw was able to recapture the riding. On his defeat in 1940, Mitchell retired from politics.

Harry Andrew Moore
Progressive Conservative for Wetaskiwin 1962-1972

Born at Wetaskiwin in 1914, he was educated at Wetaskiwin, Camrose normal school and the University of Alberta. He is a successful dairy farmer. First elected to the Commons in 1962. He was re-elected in the general elections of 1963, 1965, and 1968. In 1972 he failed to be re-nominated as the Conservative candidate. Religion: United Church.

Carl Olof Nickle
Progressive Conservative for Calgary South 1951-1957

He was born at Winnipeg in 1914. His father's family came to America in 1842 from Ireland while his mother's family originally came from Sweden. Educated at Calgary's Mount Royal College, he started his own business in 1937 as publisher of Daily Oil Bulletin and a weekly publication, Oil in Canada. Nickel entered federal politics in a by-election caused by the death of Arthur Smith. He ran as a Progressive Conservative candidate for the Calgary South riding and won. He held the seat for six years before retiring from politics. Religion: Anglican.

Steven Eugene Paproski

Progressive Conservative for Edmonton Centre 1968-1979

Progressive Conservative for Edmonton North 1979-1993

Born at Lwow, Poland, in 1928. He was of Ukrainian descent. He was educated in Edmonton, the University of North Dakota, University of Arizona and Banff School of Advanced Management. He was a general sales manager. He was first elected to Parliament in 1968 for the urban constituency of Edmonton Centre in a four-way contest. Former mayor William Hawrelak ran as an Independent Liberal candidate and thus split the Liberal vote. His brother, Dr. Ken Paproski, is the Progressive Conservative member for Edmonton Kingsway in the Alberta Legislature. He died December 2, 1993 at the age of 65. Religion: Roman Catholic

Rene-Antoine Pelletier
Social Credit for Peace River 1935-1940

Born at St. Faustin, Quebec, in 1908. He was the son of Paul Z. Pelletier and Odila St. Jean, both French Canadians. He was a grandnephew of the late Justice Pelletier of the Supreme Court of Quebec. Pelletier was educated at Montreal and Calgary, and worked as the station agent at Falher in the Peace River district of northern Alberta. He was an unsuccessful candidate in the 1935 provincial election. The same year he was the Social Credit candidate for the large Peace River riding and was successful in defeating the incumbent D.M. Kennedy. Liberal lawyer J.H. Sissons defeated him in 1940. Religion: Roman Catholic.

Eric Joseph Poole

Social Credit for Red Deer 1935-1940

Born at Northwich, Cheshire, England, in 1907. He was the son of Oswald James Poole and Helen Igo, both British. He was educated at Hennington Park, Northwich, before coming to Canada in 1909. However, he did not remain in this country for long but returned to the United Kingdom. He returned to Canada in 1928 when he established Poole Construction, which is today one of the largest construction firms in western Canada. He entered federal politics in 1935 as a Social Credit candidate for Red Deer. He won the seat. Poole did not seek re-election five years later but retired permanently from politics. Religion: Roman Catholic.

George Prudham

Liberal for Edmonton West 1949-1957

Minister of Mines 1950-1957

Born in Kilbride Ontario, in 1904, of British descent. His mother, Anna Pickett, was descended from United Empire Loyalists. He was educated at Waterdown, Ontario, and Hamilton Technical School. He became a wealthy building supply dealer, and was named president of the National House Builders Association of Canada. He was first elected to the Commons in 1949 and was named to the federal cabinet the next year. He did not have a distinguished political career, and retired from the federal arena in 1957. He died August 24, 1974 at the age of 70. Religion: United Church.

Victor Quelch

Social Credit for Acadia 1935-1958

Born at Georgetown, British Guiana, in 1891, he was the son of British parents. He was educated in the United Kingdom at Fulneck College, Leeds, before coming to Canada in 1909. He joined the Canadian army five years later and saw active duty on the Western Front. He was awarded the MC in September 1918. Upon his return he became a farmer. Quelch entered federal politics in 1935 when he captured the large central Alberta riding of Acadia from United Farmer incumbent Robert Gardiner. Quelch held the constituency until 1958 when he retired from politics. He died in 1975 at the age of 83. Religion: Anglican.

Major Daniel Lee Redman
Unionist for Calgary East

Born at Oil City, Ontario, in 1889, he was of English descent. He was educated at King's College, London, the Inns of Court, and the University of Manitoba where he obtained a law degree. He then settled in Calgary where he joined the law firm of Lougheed, Bennett and McLean. He became the director of several companies including Calgary Gas, Western Canada Natural Gas, and Alliance Power Company. He joined the Canadian Expeditionary Force in 1914, and saw active service on the Western Front. He was wounded at St. Julien in 1915. Redman entered politics in 1917 as a unionist candidate and served one term as a Member of Parliament for the city of Calgary. Redman was not a candidate in 1921. He died April 8, 1948 at the age of 58.

Harris George Rogers
Progressive Conservative for Red Deer 1958-1962

Born at Newton Robinson, Ontario, in 1891, the son of Morrison Rogers and Elizabeth Campbell, both Canadians of British descent. He was educated at Cockstown and Gradford, Ontario. He was a farmer in the Red Deer district. He saw active military service in both the Great War and the Second World War. He was awarded the Military Cross for bravery while serving with a Calgary tank regiment. He was a Tory candidate in the 1957 federal election but was defeated. The next spring he carried the riding in the Diefenbaker landslide. He was defeated in 1962 by the Social Credit National Leader at the time, Robert Thompson. Religion: United Church.

George Henry Ross

Liberal for Calgary East 1940-1945

Summoned to the Senate in 1948.

(See: List of Senators)

Percy John Rowe

Social Credit for Athabasca 1935-1940

Born at Bowmanville, Ontario in 1893, the son of Roger Rowe and Lura Allin, both Canadians. He was educated at Port Hope, Ontario. He was trained as an accountant. When he came west as a young man he worked for nine years for the Standard Bank of Canada. He was the Mundare Branch manager from 1916 to 1919. Rowe was all his life interested in economics and banking and became a disciple of Major Douglas, the "father" of Social Credit. He was the secretary-treasurer of the town of Beverly from 1922 to 1933. Rowe entered federal politics in 1935 as the Social Credit candidate for Athabasca. He won the seat, defeated Conservative lawyer Davies. He was defeated in the 1940 general election by Liberal Joseph Dechene. Religion: United Church.

Stanley Stanford Schumacher

Progressive Conservative for Palliser 1968-1979

Born at Hanna, Alberta in 1933. He was educated at Drumheller, Calgary, and at the University of British Columbia (B.Com., L.L.B degrees). He served as an officer with the RCAC before establishing his law practice at Drumheller. He entered federal politics for the first time in 1968 when he had a close to 8,000 vote majority in the newly named Palliser constituency. Religion: Anglican.

Frederick Davis Shaw

Social Credit for Red Deer 1940-1958

Born at Cardston in 1909, he was of United Empire Loyalist stock. Educated at Cardston and Calgary normal school, he became a schoolteacher at Innisfail, Alberta. Shaw entered federal politics in 1940 when he became the Social Credit candidate for the Red Deer constituency. He was successful and sat in the House of Commons for the next eighteen years. Harris Rogers defeated him in the Diefenbaker landslide of March 1958. He died on September 9, 1977. Religion: United Church.

Hugh Murray Shaw

Unionist for Macleod 1917-1921

Born at Kintore, Ontario, in 1876, he was of British descent. He was educated at Kintore, High River and Calgary after coming west with his parents in 1901. He married Annie Warren of Nanton in 1904. He became a successful farmer in the Nanton district and served on the municipal and school boards. He was elected in 1917 as Unionist member for Macleod. He was defeated four years later byU.F.A.George Coote. He died in April 1934, at Calgary.

Joseph Tweed Shaw

Labor for Calgary West 1921-1925

Born at Port Arthur, Ontario, in 1883, he was educated at Calgary and the University of Michigan where he obtained a Bachelor of Law degree. He served in the Canadian Expeditionary Force on the Western Front during the Great War. When he returned he entered federal politics and practiced law. He won one of the two urban ridings as a Labour candidate but was defeated in his re-election bid four years later. He then turned to provincial politics and was elected as a Liberal for Bow Valley in the 1926 general election. Shaw served one term in the Legislature as the leader of the opposition. He retired from politics in 1930. He died in July 1944, at Calgary. Religion: Presbyterian.

Arthur Lewis Sifton

Chief Justice of the Northwest Territories 1903-1905

Chief Justice of Alberta 1905-1910

Premier of Alberta 1910-1917

Minister of the Interior 1917-1921

Unionist for Medicine Hat 1917-1921

Born at St. John's, near London, Ontario, 1858, he was the elder son of the Honorable John Wright Sifton. Clifford Sifton Minister of the

Interior in Laurier's cabinet was his younger brother. He was educated in Winnipeg and at Victoria University, Coburg (B.A. 1880, M.A. 1888). He was called to the Bar of the Northwest Territories in 1883 and started to practice law in Brandon. He was named a Queen's Councilor in 1892, by which time he was practicing law in Calgary. Entering politics as a Liberal, he represented Banff in the territorial legislature 1899-1903, and served as Treasurer and Commissioner of Public Works in the Haultain administration. In 1903 he was named Chief Justice of the Supreme Court of the Northwest Territories and on the creation of the province of Alberta two years later he became its first Chief Justice. In 1910 he retired from the bench to become Alberta's second Premier. Besides being Premier, he was Provincial Treasurer, Minister of Public Works, and Minister of Railways and Telephones. He represented Vermillion in the Legislature. In 1917, after leading his party successfully through a provincial election, he resigned his seat in order to enter federal politics. He had broken with Laurier over the conscription issue and ran successfully in the 1917 federal election as a Unionist candidate in Medicine Hat. He was named to Borden's national government as Minister of Customs. He was one of Canada's delegates to be sent to the peace conference at Versailles in 1919. In 1920 he was named Secretary of State. He died in January, 1921, at the age of sixty-two. Professor L.G. Thomas in The Liberal Party in Alberta (1959) says that a "...fondness for the good things of life, cigars among them, did not redeem the lack of geniality that chilled his political allies and affronted his opponents." Sifton ruled the Liberal Party in Alberta with an iron hand and it is difficult to avoid the conclusion that it was his vigorous personality that saved the party from the disaster that threatened it during the Alberta and the Great Waterways episode. Although he could hold the party together while in office, he could not heal the divisions that the crisis had only deepened. Once the "the Czar" had abdicated, the Alberta Liberal party began to disintegrate. He died while still representing Medicine Hat in 1921.

John Howard Sissons

Liberal for Peace River 1940-1945

Born at Orillia, Ontario, in 1892, he was of British descent. In the early 17th century, his ancestors, who were French Huguenots, left France and settled in England. His mother was Jessie Livingstone, a cousin of the famous African explorer, Dr. David Livingstone. His father was the chief attendant at the Orillia Mental Asylum for thirty-five years. Sissons was educated at Queen's University where he obtained a Bachelor of Arts degree. He taught in small-town schools in Alberta for a couple of years while working his way through university. He studied law in Edmonton and was called to the Alberta Bar in 1921. He practiced law for twenty-five years at Grande Prairie in the Peace River county. He was always active in politics and was named the Liberal candidate for the provincial riding of Clearwater in 1920. However, this northern Alberta constituency was abolished before the 1921 Grande Prairie School Board was founded. In 1940 he entered federal politics as the Liberal candidate for Peace River. He won the seat by defeating the incumbent R.A. Pelletier. Five years later he was defeated when Solon Low, the National Leader of the Social Credit movement, won this vast northern Alberta riding. Prime Minister Mackenzie King the same year named Sisson a judge of the Southern Alberta District. When the Territorial Court of the Northwest Territories was established in 1955, be became its first judge. He retired in 1966 and was awarded an honorary degree from The University of Lethbridge in 1969, shortly before his death. He wrote his autobiography entitled Judge of the Far North in 1968.

William Skoreyko

Progressive Conservative for Edmonton East 1958-1978

Born at Edmonton 1922, he is the son of Michael Skoreyko who is of Ukrainian descent. He was educated at Edmonton and Senlac, Saskatchewan. He was a service station operator in 1958 when he was first elected to the federal house. He died September 28, 1987 at the age of 64. Religion: Greek Orthodox.

Clifford Smallwood

Progressive Conservative for Battle River-Camrose 1958-1968

Born at Irma, Alberta, in 1915, he was the son of Robert Smallwood and Margaret McKay, both of British descent. He was educated at Irma and Edmonton. He was a successful farmer in the Irma district of Alberta. Smallwood was an unsuccessful Tory candidate in the 1957 general election. However, he took the Battle River-Camrose riding in the general election that next year and held it for the next ten years. He retired from federal politics in 1968. In 1971 he entered provincial politics. He was unsuccessful, however, and Conservative party leader Peter Lougheed was able to topple the thirty-six-year-old Social Credit government. Religion: United Church.

Arthur Leroy Smith

Progressive Conservative for Calgary West 1945-1951

Born at Regina, Saskatchewan, in 1886, he was the son of Jacob Watson Smith who was of British descent. He was educated at Regina and the University of Manitoba where he obtained a Bachelor of Arts degree. In 1912 he married Sara Isabel, daughter of Thomas Ryan of Winnipeg. They had two children, a daughter and a son, Arthur Ryan.

(See: Arthur Ryan Smith, Progressive Conservative MP for Calgary South 1957-1963)

Smith established his legal practice in Calgary. He first became active in politics in 1921 when he was an unsuccessful Conservative candidate in a federal election that saw the United Farmers of Alberta and theirLabourallies take every riding in the province. Smith ran again in 1945 and was elected in Calgary West. He was re-elected four years later, but resigned his seat in the Commons in November 1951. Carl Nickle held the seat for the Tories in the resulting by-election. He died December 19, 1951. Religion: Anglican.

Arthur Ryan Smith

Progressive Conservative for Calgary South 1957-1963

Born at Calgary in 1919, he was the son of Arthur Leroy Smith, a Calgary lawyer who sat in the Commons as a Progressive Conservative during the 1940's. He was educated at Shawnigan School, British Columbia. He joined the Royal Canadian Air Force during the WWII and saw active service in Europe. He was awarded the Distinguished Flying Cross in 1944. Smith became an executive in the petroleum industry. He first became interested in civic politics, serving a three-year term on the Calgary city council. In 1955 he was one of the three Tories elected to the Legislature. Two years later he resigned his seat in order to enter federal politics. He, with fellow Calgarian Douglas Harkness and Edmonton lawyer Marcel Lambert were the only Conservatives elected in 1957 that saw Diefenbaker form a minority government. He was re-elected in the 1958 federal election with one of the largest majorities in the whole of Canada. He had a 22,442 vote majority over his nearest rival. He retired from politics in 1963. He sat in the Commons for six years before retiring from federal politics to return to industry at the age of forty-six. Religion: Anglican.

James Alexander Smith

Social Credit for Battle River-Camrose 1955-1958

Born at Bawlf, Alberta, in 1911, he was the son of Thomas D. Smith, who was of British descent. He was educated at Czar, Edmonton, the University of Alberta, and Montana State University at Missoula. Smith taught in several schools in Alberta from 1932-1955, including Czar, Paradise Valley and Kitscoty. He was the president of the Alberta Teachers' Association (ATA) for one term. Smith entered federal politics as a Social Crediter in 1955 when he ran in the by-election in Battle River-Camrose caused by the death of the sitting Member Social Crediter Robert Fair. He was successful and was re-elected two years later but was unable to hold the seat against the Diefenbaker tide in 1958. Religion: United Church.

Alfred Speakman

UFA for Red Deer 1921-1935

Born at Dundee, Scotland, in 1880, he was the son of James Speakman and Mary Hanna Farrar. He arrived in Canada with his parents as a child in 1891. He was a successful farmer in the Red Deer district for many years and was active in the UFA. He entered federal politics as a candidate in 1921 general election and sat for a total of fourteen years in Parliament. He was defeated in the Social Credit sweep of 1935. Speakman came out of retirement to run as an Independent in the 1940 provincial election. He won the provincial constituency of Red Deer and died while still an MLA in November 1943, at Edmonton. Religion: United Church.

James Stanley Speakman

Progressive Conservative for Wetaskiwin 1958-1962

Born at Penhold, Alberta, in 1906. He was the son of James Farrar

Speakman and Eva Richards, both of British descent. He was a relation of Alfred Speakman. He was educated at Victoria High School, Edmonton, and became a general accountant in Wetaskiwin. Speakman served as an officer in the Canadian Army from 1943 to 1957. He was an unsuccessful candidate in the June 1957 election, but was victorious in March 1958, when the province went completely Conservative. He died while still an MP on April 1962. Religion: United Church.

Henry Elvins Spencer

UFA for Battle River 1921-1935

Born near Alcester, England, in 1882. He worked in a bank prior to going to France in 1906 where he worked in the publishing business. He came to Canada in 1908 where he homesteaded in the Edgerton district. He became a successful farmer and was active in the UFA, being the director for Battle River from 1917 to 1921. He died October 1, 1972 at the age of 90.

Dr. George Douglas Stanley

Conservative for Calgary East 1930-1935

Born at Exter, Ontario, in 1876. He was the son of Thomas Stanley and Hannah Westman, both Canadians. His father was a former mayor of St. Mary's, Ontario. He was educated at St. Mary's Collegiate and the University of Toronto where he obtained a degree in medicine. After graduation, Stanley came west to Calgary where he became a prominent physician and stalwart prohibitionist. He became interested in provincial politics and ran unsuccessfully as a Conservative in the 1909 general election. He was victorious on his second attempt four years later when he was elected to the High River constituency. He was re-elected in 1917 and was the most fervent Conservative crusader for temperance in the Legislature, claiming that judges were drunk in hotel corridors at night and the following morning sat in judgment on those on trial for breaches of the Liquor Act. He retired from provincial politics in 1921 after becoming the president of the Alberta College of Physicians and Surgeons. He entered federal politics in 1930 when he was elected the Conservative Member for the urban riding of Calgary East with a large 5,342 vote majority. For years Dr. Stanley was next to R.B. Bennett was one of the most important Conservatives in the province. He died February 1954. Religion: United Church.

Peter Stefura

Social Credit for Vegreville 1957-1958

Born at Chipman, Alberta in 1923. He was the son of William Stefura and Helen Diduck, both Ukrainians. He was educated at Hilliard, Chipman and at the Edmonton normal school. He was a farmer in the Chipman district. Stefura was a councilor and reeve of the municipal district of Lamont. He entered federal politics as a Social Crediter in 1957 when he was elected in the Vegreville riding. He was defeated in the next federal election held nine months later by Conservative Frank Fane. Religion: Ukrainian Greek Orthodox.

Charles Stewart

Premier of Alberta 1917-1921

Liberal for Argenteuil (Quebec) 1922-1925

Liberal for Edmonton West 1925-1935

Minister of the Interior and of Mines 1921-1935

Minister of the Interior 1936-1930

Born at Strabane, Ontario, in 1868. He was of British descent. Educated at Strabane, he came to the Northwest Territories at the turn of the century and homesteaded in the Killam district of Alberta. He became a successful farmer. Elected by acclamation to the Legislature in 1909 as the Liberal Member for Sedgewick, he held the central Alberta riding until he resigned in order to enter federal politics in 1922. Stewart rose rapidly in the government of Premier Sifton, serving successively as Minister of Municipal Affairs and Minister of Public Works. When Sifton resigned to become a member of Robert Borden's Union cabinet in 1917, Stewart was chosen to become the third Premier of Alberta. He also held the post of Minister of Railways and Telephones. Despite his popularity as an individual, the United Farmers of Alberta in the 1921 general election defeated his government. He first resigned the premiership and then his seat in the Legislature. As a result of the 1921 election, not a single Liberal was elected in Alberta. Prime Minister Mackenzie King appointed Stewart to his cabinet and found him a safe seat in Quebec to run in order to admit him into the federal House. He was returned for Edmonton West in the 1925 election and retained the seat until 1935. He retired from active politics that year at the age of sixty-seven. The next year he was appointed Canadian chairman of the International Joint Commission and held this office until his death ten years later. He died in December, 1946, at Ottawa. Religion: Anglican.

John Smith Stewart

MLA for Lethbridge 1911-1925

Conservative for Lethbridge 1930-1935

Born at Brampton, Ontario, in 1878. He was the son of John Stewart and Mary Armstrong, both Canadians. He was educated at the University of Toronto where he obtained a dental degree in 1903. Prior to that he had seen active service in the Boer War as a private in Strathcona's Horse. For more than half a century he was one of the leading dentists in Lethbridge. He also had a distinguished military career. During the Great War he was awarded the BSO and the Croix de Guerre. He rose to the rank of general. Stewart was first elected to the Alberta Legislature in 1911 as a Conservative. He sat in the provincial House for fourteen years. In 1921 he refused to become the Speaker. In 1925 he failed in his first attempt to get elected to the Commons. However, five years later he was successful and represented Lethbridge in Ottawa for give years. He died in 1970. Religion: United Church.

Allen Sulatycky

Liberal for Rocky Mountain 1968

Born at Hafford, Saskatchewan, in 1938. He was of Ukrainian descent. He was educated at Hafford and the University of Saskatchewan with a B.A. and L.L.B. After graduation, he established his law practice at Whitecourt, Alberta. He entered federal politics in 1967 when he stood as the Liberal candidate in the Jasper-Edson by-election caused when Dr. Hugh Horner resigned his seat in Parliament to enter provincial politics but was defeated by Conservative Doug Caston. He ran the next year in the general election in the new-created constituency of Rocky Mountain, which includes the National Parks of Waterton,

Banff and Jasper. This was a six-way contest. Caston, who was running as an Independent Conservative, split the Conservative vote. Religion: Greek Orthodox.

Peter Talbot

Liberal for Strathcona 1904-1906

Summoned to the Senate in 1906

(See: List of Senators)

Ray Thomas

Social Credit for Wetaskiwin 1949-1958

Born at Mirror, Alberta, in 1917. He was the son of George Melvin Thomas, of Welsh descent and Zella Ray, his American wife. Educated at Mirror and Mount Royal College, Calgary, he served five years with the Royal Canadian Navy during the Second World War. He returned to become a merchant in Wetaskiwin. Thomas entered federal politics in 1949 when he was the Social Credit candidate for the central Alberta riding of Wetaskiwin. He was elected by a narrow 683 vote majority. He represented the constituency in the Commons for the next nine years before being defeated by Conservative James Speakman in 1958. Religion: United Church.

Robert Norman Thompson

Social Credit for Red Deer 1962-1968

National Social Credit Leader 1961-1968

Progressive Conservative for Red Deer 1968

Born at Duluth, Minnesota, in 1914. He was the son of Theodore Thompson and Hannah Olufson, both Canadians. He was educated at Garbutt's Business College, Calgary normal school Palmer College, Bob Jones University and the University of British Columbia. He was active in 1935 in Manitoba on behalf of the Social Credit movement. At the outbreak of the Second World War Thompson joined the Canadian Air Force and saw active service in the Middle East. In 1945 he was the director of the Imperial Ethiopian Air Force training program. He later became the Minister of

Education for Ethiopia and worked in that African nation in the field of education for fifteen years before returning to Canada in 1960. On his return he was elected president of the Social Credit Association of Canada. It was while he was the Socred national leader that the party elected thirty members to the House of Commons, four from western Canada and twenty-six from Quebec. He was elected in the central Alberta riding of Red Deer. In 1968 he changed his political affiliation and joined the Conservatives. He was re-elected that year as a Tory. He was an expert on African affairs, and referred to himself as an educator. In 1972 he announced his move to British Columbia and did not seek re-election. He died November 16, 1997. Religion: Protestant.

Syd Thompson

Social Credit MP for Edmonton-Strathcona 1957-1958

Born in Athabasca in 1920. He was educated at Rabbit Hill, Alberta. After brief employment as a banker, he joined the RCAF and saw active service during the Second World War. When he returned from the war he became the manager of a large food market in South Edmonton. He entered federal politics in 1957 and was a successful Social Credit candidate. In the next general election nine months later he was defeated by Conservative Terry Nugent.

Stanley G. Tobin

Liberal for Wetaskiwin 1925-1926

Born at Bridgewater, Nova Scotia, in 1871, and was of British descent. He was educated at Bridgewater Academy before going to the Pictour Academy. He trained as a schoolteacher and taught for several years in Alberta before he entered business. He became interested in provincial politics in 1913 when he was elected the Liberal member of the Legislature for Leduc. He was able to hold his seat when the United Farmers came to power in 1921. In 1925 he resigned his seat in the Legislature to run federally for the Wetaskiwin riding. He was successful, but was defeated by William Irvin in the general election of 1926. He died June 12, 1948 at the age of 77.

Thomas Mitchell March Tweedie
Conservative-Unionist for Calgary West 1917-1921

Born at River John, Nova Scotia, in 1871. He was of British descent. His father was a Methodist minister. He was educated at Pictour Academy, Mount Allison University, and Harvard University with a B.A. and L.L.B. He established his law practice in Calgary at the turn of the century. Tweedie first entered provincial politics in 1911, in a by-election held to fill the vacancy caused by the resignation of R.B. Bennett when he ran in the federal election that year. He remained in the Legislature until 1917 when he, too, ran federally as a Conservative-Unionist candidate. Tweedie had the largest majority in the province. He served one term in Ottawa and was not a candidate in 1921. Prime Minister Meighan appointed him a judge the same year. In 1944, he was named Chief Justice of the Trial Division of the Supreme Court of Alberta. He died in October 1944, at Lethbridge. Religion: Methodist.

David E. Warnock
Liberal for Macleod 1911-1917

Born at Hamilton, Lanarkshire, Scotland, in 1865. He was educated at Hamilton Grammar School and Glasgow Veterinary College before coming to Canada. A veterinary surgeon and farmer, he was the Dominion veterinary inspector from 1904 to 1909. He entered provincial politics in 1909, when he was the successful Liberal candidate in the Pincher Creek riding. He resigned his seat in the Legislature two years later in order to enter federal politics, and run in the Macleod constituency. He won the election, and did not seek a second term in the next federal election six years later. While he was in the Legislature, Warnock was one of the leading "insurgent" Liberals against Alberta and Great Waterways Railway contracts in the debate that resulted in Premier Rutherford quitting. Warnock moved to British Columbia in 1919 when he became the Deputy Minister of Agriculture until 1928. He died by drowning on August 1932, in the Straits of Georgia. Religion: Presbyterian.

Daniel Webster Warner
UFA Strathcona 1921-1925

Born at Richland, Iowa, United States, in 1957. He was the son of Gideon Webster and Matilda, his wife, who were both Americans. He was educated at public school in Iowa and Nebraska before he came north into Canada at the turn of the century. Warner became a farmer and stock raiser in the district south of Edmonton. He became the director of the Edmonton city dairy and the Edmonton Exhibition Company. He was active for many years in the United Farmers movement. In 1917 he received the Liberal nomination to contest the Battle River riding, however Conservative W.J. Blair defeated him. Four years later he ran in the Strathcona riding as the official United Farmers of Alberta candidate and was elected. He sat in the federal House only for one term. He died in May 1933, at Edmonton. Religion: Methodist.

John William Welborn

Liberal for Jasper-Edson 1949-1953

Born at Edmonton in 1900. He was the son of G.J. Welborn, a Canadian. He was educated at Winterburn, Edmonton, and at the Vermillion Agricultural College. In 1927 he married Muriel, daughter of W.G. Talbot of Edmonton. Welborn was a successful farmer. He entered federal politics in 1945 when he was an unsuccessful Liberal candidate. Four years later he was elected to the Commons on his second attempt for the large rural riding of Jasper-Edson. He was defeated in the 1953 general election when Socred Yuill won the seat. Religion: United Church.

William Henry White

Liberal for Victoria 19081-1921

Born at View City, Ontario, in 1865. He was educated at Ottawa. He came west as a young man in 1881 to join the North West Mounted Police. He served six years with the force before homesteading in the Fort Saskatchewan district. He entered federal politics in 1908 as a Liberal candidate. He was successful and was re-elected in 1911 and 1917. In the later election, White was one of the two Laurier Liberal to be elected in Alberta, Buchanan of Lethbridge was the other. He died in June, 1930, at Alberta- Saskatchewan. Religion: Anglican.

Eldon Woolliams

Progressive Conservative for Bow River 1958-1968

Progressive Conservative for Calgary North 1968-1980

Born at Rosetown, Saskatchewan, in 1916. He was the son of Frank Woolliams who was of British descent. He was educated at a rural school in Saskatchewan and at the University of Saskatchewan where he obtained a degree in law. He was called to the Saskatchewan Bar in 1944 and to the Alberta Bar eight years later. He was named a Queen's Councilor in 1964. He was active in politics in his native province before he came to Alberta in the early 1950's. His first attempt to obtain a seat in the Commons in 1957 was unsuccessful. However, in the federal election called by Prime Minister Diefenbaker nine months later, he won the Bow River riding for the Tories by defeating incumbent Social Crediter Johnston. He was re-elected in the 1962, 1963, 1975, and 1968 federal elections, the last for the urban riding of Calgary north. He died September 24, 2001. Religion: Anglican.

William Duncan McKay Wylie

Social Credit for Medicine Hat 1945-1957

Born at Kirriemuir, Forfarshire, Scotland, in 1900, he came to Canada as a boy in 1913 and was educated in Scotland and at Lougheed, Alberta. He worked for years as a provincial civil servant, first for the Department of Agriculture and then for the Department of Municipal Affairs as an inspector. Wylie entered federal politics in 1945 when he was the Social Credit candidate for Medicine Hat. Wylie defeated the incumbent Liberal Dr. Fred Gershaw and held the constituency until he retired in 1957. Religion: United Church.

Paul Yewchuk

Progressive Conservative for Athabasca 1968-1980

Born in 1937 in Lac La Biche, Alberta. He was the son of Jon Yewchuk, who came to Canada as a child. Educated at Lac La Biche and the University of Alberta, he was granted a medical degree in 1962. He then established his practice in Lac La Biche. Dr. Yewchuk entered federal politics in 1968 when he ran as a Conservative candidate in the large northern Alberta riding of Athabasca. He won the three-way struggle with a twelve hundred vote majority. In doing so, he defeated former provincial Liberal leader and mayor of Athabasca, Mike Maccagno. In 1971 Dr. Yewchuk, with the help of a young Irish doctor, Desmond Dwyer, set up his own northern flying doctor service. The service, using one airplane, now operates out of Fort McMurray.

Charles Yuill
Social Credit for Jasper-Edson 1953-1968

Born at Calabogie, Ontario in 1889, he was the son of John Yuill and Laurel Bailey. He was educated at Calabogie and Edmonton before becoming a merchant in the town of Barrhead, Alberta. Yuill was elected the mayor of Barrhead for seven terms before he entered federal politics in 1953 as the Social Credit candidate for Jasper-Edson. He was successful on his first attempt to enter the Commons by defeating Liberal incumbent John Welbourn. He was re-elected in 1957, but was defeated at the hands of Conservative Dr. Hugh Horner in the 1958 Diefenbaker sweeper of the province. He was unsuccessful in his attempt to unseat Horner in the 1962 federal election.

Senators from The Province of Alberta In Order of Appointment

According to the Alberta Act, which created the province in 1905, the newly-created province had the right to have four Senators.

James Lougheed, of Calgary, Conservative (1888-1925)

Phillippe Roy, of Edmonton, Liberal (1906-1911)

Peter Talbot, of Lacombe, former Liberal MP for Alberta (1906-1919)

Dr. L. George DeVeber, of Lethbridge, former Liberal MLA (1906-1925)

Amedee Forget, of Banff, Liberal (1911-1923)

The number of Senators from Albert was increased to six in 1915.

Edward Michener, of Red Deer, former Conservative MLA (1918-1948)

W.J. Harmer, of Edmonton (1918-1948)

W.A. Griesbach, of Edmonton, former Conservative MP (1921-1944)

J.L. Cote, of Edmonton, former Liberal MLA (1923-1924)

William A. Buchanan, of Lethbridge, former Liberal MLA and MP (1925-1954)

P.E. Lessard, of St. Paul, former Liberal MLA (1924-1931)

Daniel E. Riley, of High River, Liberal (1926-1948)

Pat Burns, of Calgary, Independent (1931-1936)

Dr. Aristide Blais of Edmonton, Liberal (1940-1963)

Dr. Frederick Gershaw, of Medicine Hat, former Liberal MP (1945-1963)

G.H. Ross, of Calgary, former Liberal MP (1948-1958)

James A. MacKinnon, of Edmonton, former Liberal MP (1949-1958)

J. Wesley Stambaugh, of Bruce, Liberal (1949-1963)

Donald Cameron, of Banff, Independent Liberal (1955- 1987)

James Gladstone, of Lethbridge, Independent Conservative (1958-1971)

John A. Buchanan, of Edmonton, Progressive Conservative (1958-1965)

Harry Hays, former Liberal MP (1966-1982)

Earl Hastings, of Calgary, Liberal (1966-1996)

J. Harper Prowse, former Liberal MLA (1966-1976)

Ernest C. Manning, of Edmonton, Social Credit (1970-1983)

What's in a Name?

Name	Riding	Profession
Herbert Bealey Adshead	Calgary East	Farmer, Teacher
Patrick Harvey Ashby	Edmonton East	Farmer, rancher
Gerald William Baldwin	Peace River	Barrister, lawyer
Harold Raymond Ballard	Calgary South	Business executive, chartered accountant
Richard Bedford Bennett	Calgary	Barrister, lawyer, teacher
Hilliard Harris William Beyerstein	Camrose	Chiropractor
Frederick Jack Bigg	Athabasca, Pembina	Lawyer, RCMP sergeant
John Horn Blackmore	Lethbridge	School principal, teacher
William John Blair	Battle River	Mining engineer, teacher
Kenneth Alexander Blatchford	Edmonton East	Insurance broker
Edwin William "Ted" Brunsdent	Vegreville, Medicine Hat	Farmer, Agricultural Agent
William Ashbury Buchanan	Lethbridge	Journalist, publisher
John Francis Buckley	Athabasca	Barrister
Ambrose Upton Gledstanes Bury	Edmonton East	Barrister

Cora Taylor Casselman	Edmonton East	Teacher
Frederick Clayton Casselman	Edmonton East	Barrister, teacher
Douglas Marmaduke Caston	Jasper-Edson	Newspaper publisher
Percy Griffith Davies	Athabasca	Barrister
Donald Watson Davis	Alberta, N.W.T.	Merchant
Frederick Davis	Calgary East	-
John Decore	Vegreville	Barrister, lawyer, teacher
James McCrie Douglas	Strathcona	Businessman, farmer, merchant
Manley Justin Edwards	Calgary West	Barrister, teacher
Robert Fair	Battle River	Farmer
Frank John William Fane	Vegreville	Farmer
Robert Gardiner	Medicine Hat	-
Edward Joseph Garland	Bow River	Farmer
Dr. Frederick Gershaw	Medicine Hat	Physician
General William Antrobus	Edmonton West	Lawyer
Deane Roscoe Gundlock	Lethbridge	Farmer

Dr. William Samuel Hall	Edmonton East	Dentist
Howard Hadden Halladay	Bow River	Farmer, insurance agent
R.F.L. "Dick" Hanna	Edmonton Strathcona	Teacher
Rev. Ernest George Hansell	Macleod	Clergyperson, minister
Douglas Harkness	Calgary North, Calgary Centre	Farmer, teacher
Dr. Hu Harries	Edmonton Strathcona	Economist
William Hayhurst	Vegreville	Farmer, principal, teacher
Anthony Hlynka	Vegreville	Journalist, publisher
Ambrose Holowach	Edmonton East	Business manager, businessman
Dr. Hugh MacArthur Horner	Jasper-Edson	Physician, surgeon
John Henry "Jack" Horner	Acadia	Farmer, rancher
William Irvine	Calgary East	Author, clergyperson, editor, farmer, journalist, organizer, publicist
Norman Jaques	Wetaskiwin	Farmer
Lincoln Henry Jelliff	Lethbridge	Farmer, insurance advisor, lawyer
Charles Edward Johnston	Bow River	Teacher

Donald Ferdinand Killner	Edmonton East, Athabasca	Farmer
Donald Macbeth Kennedy	Edmonton West	Farmer
Orvis Alexander Kennedy	Edmonton East	Salesman
Dr. Lawrence Elliott Kindt	Macleod	Economist, farmer
John Charles Landeryou	Calgary East	Chef
Solon Earl Low	Peace River	Farmer, gentleman, school principal, teacher
William Thomas Lucas	Camrose	Farmer
Marcel Lambert	Edmonton West	Lawyer
Michael Luchkovich	Vegreville	Teacher
Albert Frederick MacDonald	Edmonton East	Cashier, railway employee
Henry Arthur Mackie	Edmonton East	Lawyer
James Angus MacKinnon	Edmonton West.	Manager, teacher
Charles Alexander Magrath	Medicine Hat	Land surveyor
Frank Oliver	Alberta, N.W.T., Edmonton	Journalist
Horace Andrew "Bud" Olson	Medicine Hat	Farmer, merchant, rancher
Patrick Morgan Mahoney	Calgary South	Businessman, lawyer

James Alexander Marshall	Camrose	Secretary, teacher
Donald Frank Mazankowski	Vegreville	Businessman
Maitland Stewart McCarthy	Calgary	Lawyer
Dr. Wilbert McIntyre	Strathcona	Physician
Archibald Huge Mitchell	Medicine Hat	Farmer
Harry Andrew Moore	Wetaskiwin	Dairy farmer, teacher
Carl Olof Nickle	Calgary South	Editor, oilman, publisher
Steven Eugene Paproski	Edmonton Centre	Sales manager
Rene-Antoine Pelletier	Peace River	Station agent
Eric Joseph Poole	Red Deer	Building contractor
George Prudham	Edmonton West	Building contractor
Victor Quelch	Acadia	Farmer
Major Daniel Lee Redman	Calgary East	Lawyer
Harris George Rogers	Red Deer	Farmer
George Henry Ross	Calgary east	Barrister
Percy John Rowe	Athabasca	Accountant
Stanley Stanford Schumacher	Palliser	Barrister, lawyer

Frederick Davis Shaw	Red Deer	Teacher
Red Deer	Teacher	
Hugh Murray Shaw	Macleod	Farmer, rancher
Joseph Tweed Shaw	Calgary West	Barrister
Arthur Lewis Sifton	Medicine Hat	Lawyer
John Howard Sissons	Peace River	Barrister, judge
William Skoreyko	Edmonton East	Businessman, service station operator
Clifford Smallwood	Battle River-Camrose	Farmer
Arthur Leroy Smith	Calgary West	Barrister
Arthur Ryan Smith	Calgary South	Oil executive
James Alexander Smith	Battle River-Camrose	School principal, teacher
Alfred Speakman	Red Deer	Farmer
James Stanley Speakman	Wetaskiwin	Accountant, farmer
Henry Elvins Spencer	Battle River	Farmer, printer, publisher
Dr. George Douglas Stanley	Calgary East	Physician
Peter Stefura	Vegreville	Farmer
Charles Stewart	Edmonton West	Farmer
John Smith Stewart	Lethbridge	Dentist

Allen Sulatycky	Rocky Mountain	Barrister and solicitor, judge, lawyer
Peter Talbot	Strathcona	Farmer, school principal
Ray Thomas	Wetaskiwin	Merchant
Robert Norman Thompson	Red Deer	Chiropractor, teacher
Syd Thompson	Edmonton-Strathcona	Banker, manager
Stanley G. Tobin	Wetaskiwin	Businessman, farmer, teacher
Thomas Mitchell March Tweedie	Calgary West	Judge, Lawyer
David E. Warnock	Macleod	Farmer, veterinary surgeon
Daniel Webster Warner	Strathcona	Farmer, rancher
John William Welborn	Jasper-Edson	Farmer
William Henry White	Victoria	Farmer
Eldon Woolliams	Bow River, Calgary North	Barrister and solicitor, teacher, trial lawyer
William Duncan McKay Wylie	Medicine Hat	Farmer, public servant
Paul Yewchuk	Athabasca	Physician, surgeon
Charles Yuill	Jasper-Edson	Butcher and meat cutter, merchant

Biographies of Senators From Alberta (1905-1972)

Biographical sketches of each of the twenty-six citizens of the province who have been named to the Upper Chamber of the Canadian Parliament

Dr. Aristide Blais

From Edmonton, Liberal, Surgeon

Summoned to the Senate in 1940

He was born in 1875 at Berthier, Quebec. He was the son of Narcisse Blais and Philomene Buteau, both French-Canadians. Educated at Laval University (D.Sc., M.D.) he served as a medical officer in France during the Great War. He was the surgeon and chief surgeon at the General Hospital in Edmonton for many years. He died in 1964. Religion: Roman Catholic

John Alexander "Buck" Buchanan

From Edmonton, Progressive Conservative, Engineer

Summoned to the Senate in 1940

He was born at Comber, Ontario, in 1887 and educated there. At the University of Toronto he obtained a civil engineering degree in 1909. He worked for years in the Northwest Territories as an engineer. Later he moved to Edmonton where he became president of Buchanan Construction and Engineering Company. He was an unsuccessful Conservative candidate in the 1930 provincial election. Buchanan resigned from the Senate in October 1965. Religion: Anglican.

William Ashbury Buchanan

MLA for Lethbridge, 1909-1910

Minister without Portfolio, 1909-1911

M.P. for Medicine Hat, 1911-1917

M.P. for Lethbridge, 1917-1921

Senator from Alberta, 1925-1954

Born at Fraserville, Ontario, in 1876. The son of Rev. William Buchanan and Mary Pendrie, he commenced his long newspaper career by working as a reporter on several Ontario newspapers. In 1905 he came west and bought a half-interest in The Lethbridge Herald, a weekly. He converted it into a daily and soon became the sole owner. In 1907 he organized the first legislature library in Edmonton. He was elected to the provincial house in 1909 and was taken into the Rutherford cabinet. He was then the only cabinet minister that has ever been named from Lethbridge. Two years later he entered federal politics when he defeated the sitting member of the Medicine Hat, Charles Magrath, the first mayor of Lethbridge. He was re-elected in 1917 for the newly created Lethbridge riding. In 1925, he was named to the Senate. Under his guidance, The Lethbridge Herald acquired a widespread reputation for public and regional service, encouraging the building of railways, irrigation works, highways and public parks. Buchanan was one of the most influential Liberals in Western Canada for many years. He died in Lethbridge in 1954. Religion: Methodist.

Patrick Burns

From Calgary, Independent Conservative, Rancher

Senator from Alberta 1931-1936

Born at Oshawa, Ontario, in 1856, of Irish descent, he came west to Manitoba as a young man and went into business for himself as a cattle dealer. In 1890 he arrived in Calgary where he acquired his ranch and established a meatpacking firm. In the course of time it became one of the largest businesses of its kind in the world. In 1912 Burns, who was better known as Pat, was one of the financial backers for the first Calgary Stampede. He held directorships in a number of banking, insurance and engineering firms. He was Calgary's first industrial millionaire tycoon. Prime Minister R.B. Bennett, who had known Burns for thirty-five years, made the first non-political appointment to the Senate when he summoned the Calgarian to the Upper Chamber. He resigned his seat in 1936 and died a few months later at the age of eighty years.

Donald Cameron

From Banff, Independent Liberal, Educator

Summoned to the Senate in 1955

Born in 1903 at Devonport, England. His family came to Canada in 1906. He was the son of Donald Cameron, who was the U.F.A. member of the legislature for Innisfail from 1921 to 1935. He was educated at Lakeview and the University of Alberta (B.Sc. 1930; M. Sc. 1934). He received an LL.D. degree (Honoris Causa) from the University of British Columbia in 1959. He married Stella Mary Ewing of Calgary. Cameron was the Director of Extension, University of Alberta, for twenty years, 1936-1956, and Director of the Banff School of Fine Arts from 1936 to the present. He was the chairman of a Royal Commission on Education in Alberta in the late 1950's. He authored Campus in the Clouds. Religion: United Church.

Jean Leon Cote

From Edmonton, Liberal, Civil Engineer and Surveyor

MLA for Athabasca 1909-1913

MLA for Grouard 1913-1924

Provincial Secretary 1918-1921

Senator from Alberta 1923-1924

Born at Les Eboulements, Quebec, in 1867, he was of French Canadian descent. He was educated at the commercial academy at Montmagny, Quebec. He worked as a land surveyor for the federal Department of the Interior from 1893 to 1900. He then became the director of several companies, including Jasper Colleries, and his own mining and engineering firm. He entered provincial politics when he ran as a

Liberal candidate for Athabasca in 1909. He was elected and re-elected for the constituency of Grouard in the general elections of 1913, 1917, and 1921. He served in Premier Charles Stewart's cabinet as the Provincial Secretary from 1918 until it was defeated by the United Farmers of Alberta three years later. He was appointed to the Senate by Mackenzie King in August, 1923, but died a year later. Religion: Roman Catholic.

Dr. Leverett George DeVeber

From Lethbridge, Liberal, Physician

MLA for the Northwest Territories 1898-1905

MLA for Lethbridge 1905-1906

Minister Without Portfolio 1905-1906

Senator from Alberta 1906-1919

Born at St. John, New Brunswick, in 1848. He was of United Empire Loyalist stock. He was educated at King's College, Windsor, Nova Scotia, and Bartholomew Hospital, London, from where he graduated in 1870. He came to western Canada with the Northwest Mounted Police to which force he was named staff surgeon. He started a private practice in Macleod but moved to Lethbridge in 1890. Dr. DeVeber is among the first physicians to come to Lethbridge. He entered territorial politics as a Liberal when he was elected by acclamation to represent the area in the Regina Legislature. He was named to the first Alberta cabinet formed by Rutherford as a Minister Without Portfolio. However, within a year he was appointed to the Senate by Wilfrid Laurier. He died in July 1925. Religion: Anglican.

Amédée Emmanuel Forget

From Banff, Liberal, Lawyer

Summoned to the Senate in 1911

He was born in 1847 at Marieville, Quebec. He was called to the Bar in 1871, serving for some years as secretary of the Council of the Bar for Montreal. He then entered the Dominion civil service and was one of the commissioners for the settlement of the Metis claims in

1885 in the Northwest Territories in 1898. He still held this position when the provinces of Alberta and Saskatchewan were created by the act of the federal parliament. He was then appointed the first Lieutenant-Governor of Saskatchewan (1905-1910). Moving to Alberta, he settled at Banff whence he was named to the Upper Chamber. Forget died June 1923 at Ottawa.

Dr. Frederick W. Gershaw

From Medicine Hat, Liberal Physician

MP for Medicine Hat 1925-1935 and 1940-1945

Senator from Alberta 1945-1963

Born at Emerson, Manitoba, in 1883, he was of German descent. He was educated at Emerson and the University of Manitoba where he obtained a medical degree. He established his practice in Medicine Hat and was a popular physician for many years. He was keen on southern Alberta history, and was the author of several works. Dr. Gershaw entered federal politics in 1921 when he ran as a Liberal and failed to get elected. He was, however, successful four years later. He represented Medicine Hat in the Commons for fifteen years before he was appointed to the Senate by Mackenzie King in 1945. Religion: Lutheran.

James Gladstone

From Lethbridge, Independent Conservative, Farmer

Summoned to the Senate by Diefenbaker in 1958-1971

He had the distinction of being the first Treaty Aboriginal to be appointed to the Upper Chamber. Born in 1887 near Mountain Mill, Alberta. Son of William Gladstone, a trader, and Harriet LeBlanc who was part of the Kainai tribe, he was raised and educated at St. Paul's Anglican Missions on the Kainai Nation reserve. Married in 1911 to Janie, daughter of Potaina of the Kainai tribe, Gladstone was active for many years in the Indian Association of Alberta. He died in 1971. Religion: Anglican.

William Antrobus Griesbach

From Edmonton, Conservative, Soldier

Senator from Alberta 1921-1945

Born at Fort Qu'Appelle, Saskatchewan, in 1878, he was the son of Colonel Arthur Griesbach of the Northwest Mounted Police. He was educated at St. John's College, Winnipeg. He served in the Canadian Mounted Rifles in the South African War with General Stewart of Lethbridge and Colonel Jamieson of Edmonton – all three were active Conservatives. On his return, he was called to the Alberta Bar in 1901. Griesbach first entered civic politics. He was elected alderman in 1905 and again in 1906. He was elected mayor of Edmonton in 1907. He attempted unsuccessfully to get into the legislature in Edmonton in 1907. He also tried to get elected to the House of Commons in 1911 but was defeated. On the outbreak of the Great War he volunteered for service in the Canadian Expeditionary Force and saw active duty in France. He received rapid promotion and was awarded the DSO and Bar, CMG and CB besides being mentioned in dispatches six times. In the federal election of 1917 he was finally successful in being elected to the Commons as a member for Edmonton West. In doing so, he defeated Liberal Frank Oliver, who had served six years in Laurier's cabinet. Griesbach was trailing by eighty votes after the civilian votes had been tallied. The military votes gave him close to a 3,000-vote majority when they had been included. He was created a K.C. in 1919 and appointed to the Senate by Minister Arthur Meighan in 1921. Griesbach was named Inspector General for western Canada in 1940. He died in January, 1945, in Edmonton. His autobiography I Remember, was published by Ryerson Press in 1946. Religion: Anglican.

Richard Hardisty

From Edmonton, Conservative, Chief Factor

Senator from the Northwest Territories 1888-1889

Born in 1831, he was educated at St. John's College, Winnipeg. Hardisty, like his grandfather and father before him, was for many years Chief Factor of Hudson's Bay Company in charge of the Edmonton district. He was an unsuccessful Conservative candidate for the federal house from the Northwest Territories riding of Alberta in 1887. Sir John A. MacDonald named him to the Red Chamber a year later. However, Senator Hardisty drowned in 1887, following an accident while travelling from Prince Alberta to Qu'Appelle by wagon. His niece's husband, thirty-five year old Calgary lawyer James Lougheed, was named to the senate as his replacement.

William J. Harmer

From Edmonton, Liberal, Civil Servant

Senator from Alberta from 1918-1947

Born at Fort Frontenace (Kingston), Ontario, in 1872. He was the son of James Harmer who was of English descent. Educated at Napanee, he came west in 1891 to join the railway operating traffic department. He rose rapidly in the provincial civil service and was the Deputy Minister of Railways from 1905 until he was named to the Senate thirteen years later. The Calgary Herald referred to his appointment with disappointment:

> Mr. Harmer has performed no public action, nor has he attained any public or personal distinction... His record is that of a civil servant of very ordinary ability, whose chief and almost only function has been to act as a political manager for Hon. A.L. Sifton.

It is said that the Senator did not speak even once in the twenty-nine years he sat in the Red Chamber. He died in September 1947, at Napanese, Ontario.

Earl Adam Hastings

From Palliser-Foothills, Liberal Petroleum Landman

Senator from Alberta 1966

Born at Regina in 1924, he was educated at Wetmore and Regina College. He joined the Canadian Air Force in 1942 and saw active service in Europe. He attained the rank of pilot officer. On his return to Canada, he became the executive assistant to the leader of the

Saskatchewan Liberal party, a position he held for six years. In 1952 he joined the federal civil service, being the land administrator of the Bow River irrigation project. In 1959 he joined the Sun Oil Company and became a petroleum landman. Hastings was always interested in politics. He ran against Eldon Woolliams, PC, a Member of Parliament for Bow River in the 1962 and 1963 elections, but was defeated both times. Religion: United Church.

Harry William Hays

From Calgary, Liberal, Rancher

Senator from Alberta 1966-1982

Minister of Agriculture 1963-1965

Born at Carstairs, Alberta in 1909, he was the son of Dr. Thomas Hays and Ambriss Foster. He was educated at Glenmore and Calgary. He was a wealthy rancher. Hays was the mayor of Calgary from 1959 to 1963 when he entered federal politics. He won the Calgary South riding and was named by Prime Minister Lester Pearson to the cabinet as Minister of Agriculture. He only sat in parliament for two years before being defeated in the 1965 election. In 1966 Pearson appointed him to the Upper Chamber. Religion: Roman Catholic.

Prosper-Edmond Lessard

From St. Paul, Liberal, Broker and Merchant

Senator from Alberta 1925-1931

Born February 3, 1873 at Cranbourne, Quebec in 1873. He was elected as a Liberal Member of the Legislative Assembly for St. Paul in 1913. He was an active member of the Young Liberal's Club and the Canadian Club. He was on the local Board of Trade Council and acted as the chairperson of the retail committee. He was involved with the formation of a Young Liberal Club athletic program. From 1925 to 1931 he served in the Senate and after being appointed by Prime Minister William Lyon Mackenzie King. He died April 11, 1931 at the age of 58.

Sir James Lougheed

From Calgary, Conservative, Lawyer

Senator from Alberta 1889-1925

Born in Brampton, Ontario, in 1854. He was the son of a building contractor and as a young man he worked as a carpenter before obtaining a law degree from Osgood Hall. He was called to the Ontario Bar in 1881 and practiced briefly in Toronto before moving west. He arrived in Calgary two years later on foot and was the first lawyer to establish himself on the banks of the Bow River. In 1881 Lougheed married Belle Hardisty, daughter of William Hardisty and niece of both Senator Richard Hardisty and Lord Strathcona. When Senator Hardisty died following an accident five years later, the thirty-five year old Calgary lawyer was appointed to succeed him in the Senate. When Lougheed took his seat, was the youngest member of the Upper Chamber. In 1906 he became the opposition leader in the Senate and five years later he was brought into Borden's Conservative cabinet as Minister Without Portfolio. Later, in Prime Minister Arthur Meighen's cabinet of 1920, Senator Lougheed was the Minister of the Interior. It was said many times in his later years that he would have been Prime Minister had he been in the Commons. Premier Peter Lougheed was his grandson. Religion: Anglican.

James MacKinnon

From Edmonton, Liberal, Investment Dealer

Senator of Alberta 1949-1957

Born at Port Elgin, Ontario, in 1881. He was the son of James MacKinnon and Margaret Tolmie, both of British descent. He taught briefly in Ontario and Alberta before he settled in Edmonton where he became a reporter for The Edmonton Bulletin. In 1911 he went into the insurance business as managing director of James A. MacKinnon of which he was the president for many years. He also held directorships in several other important corporations. Entering federal politics in 1935, he ran in the Edmonton West riding which Charles Stewart had held for a number of years. He was elected and remained n the Commons until he was appointed to the Senate fourteen years later. From 1935 to 1999, Alberta did not have a representative on the federal cabinet. In the later year MacKinnon was brought into Mackenzie King's cabinet as a Minister Without Portfolio, and held successive appointments as Minister of Trade and Commerce, 1940-1948, Minister of Fisheries, 1948, and Minister of Mines and Resources, 1948-1949. From April 1949, until his resignation from the cabinet in December 1950, he was once against Minister Without Portfolio. Religion: Presbyterian.

Ernest Charles Manning

From Edmonton, Social Credit, Minister

MLA for Calgary and then Edmonton 1935-1965

Provincial Secretary 1935-1943

Minister of Trade and Industry 1935-1943

Premier of Alberta 1943-1968

Provincial Treasurer 1944-1954

Minister of Mines and Minerals 1952-1962

Attorney General 1955-1966

Senator from Alberta 1970-1983

Born at Carnduff, Saskatchewan, in 1908, he was the son of George Manning and Elizabeth Dickson. He was educated at Rosetown, Saskatchewan and the Prophetic Bible Institute in Calgary. As a young man he came under the influence of William "Bible Bill" Aberhart and was closely associated with him as teacher of fundamentalist Christianity and later as advocate of the Social Credit theory of Major Douglas. Manning ran in Calgary as a Social Credit candidate and after being elected he was taken into Aberhart's cabinet. On the Premier's death eight years later, Manning was chosen by the Social Credit members of the Legislature to be Aberhart's successor. He was the dominant figure in Alberta politics for thirty-five years. He retired from provincial politics in December 1969, after serving twenty-five years as Premier. Prime Minister Trudeau subsequently appointed him to the Senate in October 1970. He received an honorary degree from The University of Lethbridge in 1972.

(See: A.W. Cashman, Ernest C. Manning. 1958)

Edward Michener

From Red Deer, Conservative, Financial Broker

MLA for Red Deer 1909-1918

Alberta Leader of Conservative Party

Senator from Alberta 1918-1945

Born at Tintern, Lincoln County, Ontario, he was the son of Jacob Michener and Eliza Michener. He was educated at St. Catherine's Collegiate Institute, Victoria University, Toronto, and at Wesley College, Winnipeg. He married Mary Roland in 1897. They had four sons and four daughters. One of his sons, Roland Michener, was sworn in as the Governor General of Canada on April 17, 1967. Michener was a financial broker and became active in civic politics in Red Deer where he settled. He was mayor of Red Deer for two terms. He entered provincial politics in 1909 when he ran as the Conservative candidate in Red Deer. He represented this constituency in the Legislature for the next ten years. After R.B. Bennett entered federal politics in 1911, he became the leader of the Alberta Conservative party. Robert Borden appointed him to the Senate in 1918. He died in June 1947, at the age of seventy-eight years. Religion: Methodist.

J. Harper Prowse

From Edmonton, Liberal, Lawyer

Senator from Alberta 1966-1976

Born at Taber, Alberta, in 1913. He was the son of J.H. Prowse who was of British descent. He was educated at Taber and the University of Alberta where he obtained a B.A. and an LL.B. degree. He worked as a teacher (1931-1934) and as a newspaper reporter when he was a young man before joining the Canadian Army. He saw active service with the Loyal Edmonton Regiment in Italy during the Second World War, and attained the rank of captain. He was elected to the legislature in 1945 to represent Albertans who were serving in the Canadian Army. He sat as an Independent during his first term. He joined the Liberal party in 1948 and became the Liberal provincial leader, a position he held for the next ten years. He failed in his attempt to defeat Premier Manning's Social Credit administration, although he led a large opposition party following the 1955 election. He was unsuccessful in his efforts to be elected to the Commons. In 1988 he resigned as party leader to devote more time to his law practice. He ran against incumbent Marcel Lambert in Edmonton West in 1962 and 1963. Prime Minister Pearson appointed him to the Senate in 1966.

Daniel Edward Riley
From High River, Liberal Rancher
Senator from Alberta 1926-1948

Born at Baltic, Prince Edward Island, in 1860, he was educated at a normal school in Charlottetown. He moved to Alberta in 1882, and was a pioneer rancher in the High River district. He also founded the real estate and insurance firm of D.E. Riley and Sons in 1900. Six years later he was elected the first mayor of High River. Riley was an unsuccessful Liberal candidate in the 1917 general election. He was called to the Senate in 1926. He died in April 1948 at Calgary. Religion: Presbyterian.

George Henry Ross
From Calgary, Liberal, Lawyer
Senator from Alberta 1948-1958

Born at Bedeque, Prince Edward Island, in 1878 and educated at Michigan University where he obtained an LL.B. In May 1911 he married May, the daughter of David McDougall of Morley, Alberta. As a young man he settled in Calgary where he practiced law for many years. He was an unsuccessful Liberal candidate in the provincial election of 1913 but was created a K.C. In 1940 he was the Liberal candidate for the federal riding of Calgary East and defeated the incumbent Social Crediter, John Landeryou, by 485 votes. He was named to the Upper Chamber in 1948. Ross died in September 1956, at Calgary.

Dr. Phillippe Roy
From Edmonton, Liberal, Physician
Senator from Alberta 1906-1911

Born at St. Francois, Quebec, in 1868, he was the son of G.B. Roy and Josephine Vallieres, both French Canadians. He was educated at the College Ste. Anne de la Pocatiere and Laval University where he obtained a medical degree in 1889. He came west and settled in Edmonton where he developed a successful practice. He also became the managing direction of Le Courrier de l'Ouest, a French language newspaper. Dr. Roy was largely interested in extending the work and influence of French immigration and French capital to Canada. He was anti-clerical and a strong supporter of Wilfrid Laurier who was Prime Minister from 1896 to 1911. He was appointed to the Senate in 1906 as one of Alberta's new Senators. Dr. Roy resigned his seat in the Upper Chamber in 1911 upon his appointment as Commissaire General du Canada en France and took up residence in Paris. He replaced another former Senator, Hectre Fabre, who had held the post for thirty years. The status of the post was raised to that of Envoy Extraordinary and Minister Plenipotentiary to France in 1928. Roy retired in December 1938, and died ten years later at Ottawa.

J. Wesley Stambaugh

From Bruce, Liberal, Farmer

Senator from Alberta 1949-1964

Born at Melvin, Michigan, in 1888, he was the son of Rev. Alberta Stambaugh, a Methodist minister, and Christine Zimmerman. After receiving his education in the United States he came to Canada in 1905 and homesteaded in the Bruce district. In 1912 he married Amy Lake of Moscow, Ontario. He was the president of the Liberal Association of Alberta when he was called to the Senate in 1949. He retired from the Senate in 1964. Religion United Church.

Peter Talbot

From Strathcona, Liberal, Farmer

Born at Eramosa, Ontario, in 1854. He was of Scottish descent. Educated at Ottawa normal school, he obtained a first-class teaching certificate and taught at Cornwall in the 1880's before coming west. He was the principal of Macleod Public School 1890-1892 and Justice of the Peace for ten years. Talbot was elected to the Regina Parliament in 1902 as a supporter of the Haultain government. Two years later he won the newly created Strathcona riding for the Liberals. Talbot could have become the first Premier of Alberta but declined the honour. He was not a wealthy man and professed to find the hurly-burly of politics beyond his means and strength. In 1906 he was named to the Upper Chamber by Laurier as one of the new Senators from Alberta. He was fifty-two years of age at this time. Talbot died December 6, 1919, at Lacombe.

Chronological List of Alberta Chief Justices (1907-1990)

1907	Arthur Lewis Sifton
1910	Horace Harvey
1921	David Lynch Scott
1924-1949	Horace Harvey
1950	George Bligh O'Connor
1957	Clinton James Ford
1960	S. Bruce Smith
1974	William A. McGillivray
1979	James Herbert Laycroft
1990	Catherine Ann Fraser

An Alphabetical List of the Chief Justices of Alberta With a Brief Biographical Sketch

Clinton James Ford

Chief Justice of Alberta 1957-1960

Born at Corinth, Ontario, in 1882, he was educated at the University of Toronto and Osgoode Hall, Toronto, before completing his legal studies in Alberta. He was called to the Alberta Bar in 1910. Ford was named a K.C. in 1921. From 1913 to 1942 he practiced law in Calgary. In the latter year he was appointed a judge of the District Court. In 1945 he was appointed a justice of the Supreme Court of Alberta and five years later he transferred to the appellate division. On the death of Chief Justice O'Connor in January 1957, Judge Ford was named Chief Justice of Alberta. He was 75 years of age at the time. He received an honorary doctor of laws degree from the University of Alberta. Ford died in 1961.

Horace Harvey
Chief Justice of Alberta 1910-1921 and 1924-1949

Born in Elgin County, Ontario, in 1863, he was the son of William Harvey who was the Liberal Member of Parliament for Elgin East from 1872 until his death two years later. He was educated at the University of Toronto (B.A. 1886; LL.B. 1888). He was called to the Ontario Bar in 1889 before moving west. He was called to the Bar of the Northwest Territories in 1893 and established his law practice in Calgary. Harvey was successively appointed Registrar of the Land Titles for Southern Alberta in 1869, Deputy Attorney General of the Northwest Territories in 1900, and Puisne Judge of the Territorial Supreme Court in 1904. He was appointed judge of the newly organized Supreme Court of Alberta in 1907. He rose to the rank of Chief Justice on the retirement of Arthur Sifton in October 1910, when the former Chief Justice became Alberta's second Premier. Harvey was 47 years of age at the time.

On the reorganization of the courts in 1821, he became Chief Justice of the Trial Division while David Lynch Scott was named Chief Justice. Three years later on the death of Scott, he was appointed Chief Justice of the Appellate Division. Meanwhile in 1917 he had been named Chairman of the Board of Governors of the University of Alberta. This post he held until 1940.

It was in 1930 Harvey was assigned one of the most difficult tasks in his career – the problem of investigating the circumstances surround the sinking of the schooner Gypsum Queen, sunk off the west coast of Ireland allegedly after being torpedoed by a German U-boat during the Great War. He died at the advanced age of 86. He was the last of the officials carried over into Alberta from the Territorial days. Chief Justice Harvey was scholarly, studious and dignified. He had an analytical mind and always got down to the roots in hearing cases in the Trial Court or reviewing judgments in the Appellate Court. Religion: Anglican.

George Bligh O'Connor

Chief Justice of Alberta 1950-1957

Born at Brampton, Upper Canada in 1845, he was educated at the Brampton grammar school, and called to the Ontario Bar in 1870. He practiced law first in Orangeville, Ontario, and after 1882 in Regina, Northwest Territories. He was the first mayor of Regina in 1883 and organized a volunteer corps for home duty during the Red River revolt two years later. Scott was one of the Counsel for the Crown at the trial of Louis Riel. The Crown demanded the death penalty for high treason for Riel, though it has been said that the shooting of Orangeman Thomas Scott in March 1870, during the Red River Rebellion was the real reason why the Ontario Orangemen wanted Riel slain. Riel was hanged at the N.W.M.P. barracks in November 1885. The portrait of the Crown Prosecutor, David Lynch Scott, hangs in the Court House Regina today. For his services in connection with this trial, Scott was named a Q.C., and nine years later he was raised to the bench in the Northwest Territories. In 1905 he was transferred to the bench of Alberta, and on the reorganization of the courts, in 1921, was appointed Chief Justice of the province. He was seventy-six years of age at the time. He died at South Cooking Lake, Alberta, in July 1924. Religion: Anglican.

Arthur Sifton

Chief Justice of Alberta 1906-1910

(See: list of Members of Parliament)

Sidney Bruce Smith

Chief Justice of Alberta 1961

Born at Toronto in 1899, he was the son of Frederick Howard Smith and Kath Smith, nee Marks. He was educated at the University of Alberta (B.A. 1919; LL.B. 1922 – gold medalist). Bruce Smith read law with Brank Ford of Edmonton before being called to the Bar of Alberta in 1922. He practiced law in Alberta for many years. He served on the Edmonton Public School Board from 1937 to 1941. Prime Minister Diefenbaker in 1958 named him Chairman of the Board of Transport

Commissioners for Canada. A year later he was appointed judge of the Trial Division of the Supreme Court of Alberta. On the death of Chief Justice Ford, Bruce Smith was appointed Chief Justice of Alberta in February 1961. He was sixty-one years of age at the time. In 1962 he was awarded an honorary degree from the University of Alberta. Religion: Anglican.

Alberta Federal Ridings With the Names of Members of Parliament With Their Party Affiliations 1905-1972

Abbreviations:

C.	Conservative or Liberal Conservative
C.C.F.	Co-operative Commonwealth Federal Government
G.	Government (1917)
IND.	Independent
L.	Liberal
L.A.B.	Labour
N.D.	New Democracy
N.D.P.	New Democratic Party
O.	Opposition (1917)
P.	Progressive
P.C.	Progressive Conservative
S.C.	Social Credit
U.F.A.	United Farmers of Alberta

Acadia (est. 1924)
See: Medicine Hat and Bow River

1925	GARDINER, Robert (P)
1926	GARDINER, Robert (UFA)
1930	GARDINER, Robert (UFA)
1935	QUELCH, Victor (SC)
1940	QUELCH, Victor (SC)
1945	QUELCH, Victor (SC)
1949	QUELCH, Victor (SC)
1953	QUELCH, Victor (SC)
1957	QUELCH, Victor (SC)
1958	HORNER, John Henry (PC)
1962	HORNER, John Henry (PC)
1963	HORNER, John Henry (PC)
1965	HORNER, John Henry (PC)

Athabasca (est.1924)
See: Edmonton East and Battle River

1925	CROSS, Charles Wilson (L)
1926	KELLNER, Donald Ferdinand (UFA)
1930 * March 21, 1932	BUCKLEY, John Francis (L) DAVIES, Percy Griffith (C)
1935	ROWE, Percy John (SC)
1940	DECHENE, Joseph (L)

1945	DECHENE, Joseph (L)
1949	DECHENE, Joseph (L)
1953	DECHENE, Joseph (L)
1957	DECHENE, Joseph (L)
1958	BIGG, Frederick Johnstone (PC)
1962	BIGG, Frederick Johnstone (PC)
1963	BIGG, Frederick Johnstone (PC)
1965	BIGG, Frederick Johnstone (PC)
1968	YEWCHUK, Paul (PC)

Battle River (est. 1916)
See: Strathcona

1917	BLAIR, William John (G)
1921	SPENCER, Henry Elvins (P)
1925	SPENCER, Henry Elvins (P)
1926	SPENCER, Henry Elvins (P)
1930	SPENCER, Henry Elvins (P)
1935	FAIR, Robert (SC)
1940	FAIR, Robert (SC)
1945	FAIR, Robert (SC)
1949	FAIR, Robert (SC)

Battle River-Camrose

1953 *June 20, 1955	FAIR, Robert (SC) SMITH, James Alexander (SC)
1957	SMITH, James Alexander (SC)
1958	SMALLWOOD, Clifford S. (PC)
1962	SMALLWOOD, Clifford S. (PC)
1963	SMALLWOOD, Clifford S. (PC)
1965	SMALLWOOD, Clifford S. (PC)
1968	DOWNEY, Cliff (PC)

Bow River (est.1914, altered 1924)
See: Medicine Hat

1917	HALLADAY, Howard Haddan (G)
1921	GARLAND, Edward Joseph (P)
1925	GARLAND, Edward Joseph (P)
1926	GARLAND, Edward Joseph (P)
1930	GARLAND, Edward Joseph (P)
1935	JOHNSTON, Charles Edward (SC)
1940	JOHNSTON, Charles Edward (SC)
1945	JOHNSTON, Charles Edward (SC)
1949	JOHNSTON, Charles Edward (SC)

1953	JOHNSTON, Charles Edward (SC)
1957	JOHNSTON, Charles Edward (SC)
1958	WOOLLIAMS, Eldon Mattison (PC)
1962	WOOLLIAMS, Eldon Mattison (PC)
1963	WOOLLIAMS, Eldon Mattison (PC)
1965	WOOLLIAMS, Eldon Mattison (PC)

See: Palliser and Rocky Mountain House

Calgary (est. 1906-1967)

1908	McCARTHY, Maitland Stewart (C)
1911	BENNETT, Richard Bedford (C)

See: Calgary East and Calgary West

Calgary Centre (est. 1968)

1968	HARKNESS, Hon, Douglas Scott (PC)

Calgary East
See: Calgary

1917	REDMAN, Daniel Lee (G)
1921	IRVINE, William (LAB)
1925	DAVIS, Fred (C)
1926	ADSHEAD, Herbert Bealey (L)
1930	STANLEY, George Douglas (C)
1935	LANDERYOU, John Charles (SC)
1940	ROSS, George Henry (L)
1945	HARKNESS, Douglas Scott (PC)
1949	HARKNESS, Douglas Scott (PC)

See: Calgary North and Calgary South

Calgary North
See: Calgary East and Calgary West

1935	HARKNESS, Douglas Scott (PC)
1957	HARKNESS, Douglas Scott (PC)
1958	HARKNESS, Hon. Douglas Scott (PC)
1962	HARKNESS, Hon. Douglas Scott (PC)

1963	HARKNESS, Hon. Douglas Scott (PC)
1965	HARKNESS, Hon. Douglas Scott (PC)
1968	WOOLLIAMS, Eldon Mattison (PC)

Calgary South
See: Calgary East and Calgary West

1953	NICKLE, Carl Olof (PC)
1957	SMITH, Arthur R. (PC)
1958	SMITH, Arthur R. (PC)
1962	SMITH, Arthur R. (PC)
1963	HAYS, Harry William (L)
1965	BALLARD, H. Ray (PC)
1968	MAHONEY, Patrick (L)

Calgary West
See: Calgary

1917	TWEEDIE, Thomas Mitchell (G)
1921	SHAW, Joseph Tweed (LAB)
1925	BENNETT, Hon. Richard Bedford (C)

1926	BENNETT, Hon. Richard Bedford (C)
1930 *Auust 25, 1930	BENNETT, Hon. Richard Bedford (C)
1935 *September 18, 1939	BENNETT, Hon. Richard Bedford (C) CUNNINGTON, Douglas G.L. (C)
1940	EDWARDS, Manley Justin (L)
1945	SMITH, Arthur LeRoy (PC)
1949 * December 10, 1951	SMITH, Arthur LeRoy (PC) NiCKLE, Carl Olof (PC)

See: Calgary North and Calgary South

Camrose (est. 1924)
See: Red Deer and Victoria

1925	LUCAS, William Thomas (P)
1926	LUCAS, William Thomas (UFA)
1930	LUCAS, William Thomas (UFA)
1935	MARSHALL, James Alexander (SC)
1940	MARSHALL, James Alexander (ND)
1945	MARSHALL, James Alexander (SC)
1949	BEYERSTEIN, Hilliard Harris William (SC)

See: Battle River-Camrose

Crowfoot (est. 1968)

| 1968 | HORNER, John Henry (PC) |

Edmonton (est. 1906-1907)

| 1908 | OLIVER, Hon. Frank (L) |
| 1911 | OLIVER, Hon. Frank (L) |

See: Edmonton East and Edmonton West

Edmonton East
See: Edmonton

1917	MACKIE, Henry Arthur (G)
1921	KELLNER, Donald Ferdinand (P)
1925	BURY, Ambrose Upton Gledstanes (C)
1926	BLATCHFORD, Kenneth Alexander
1930	BURY, Ambrose Upton Gledstanes (C)
1935	HALL, William Samuel (SC)
*March 21, 1938	
KENNEDY, Orvis A. (SC)	

1940	CASSELMAN, Cora Taylor (L)
1945	ASHBY, Patrick Harvey (SC)
1949	HOLOWACH, Ambrose (SC)
1953	HOLOWACH, Ambrose (SC)
1957	SKOREYKO, William (PC)
1958	SKOREYKO, William (PC)
1962	SKOREYKO, William (PC)
1963	SKOREYKO, William (PC)
1965	SKOREYKO, William (PC)
1968	SKOREYKO, William (PC)

Edmonton-Strathcona

1953	HANNA, Richmond Francis Lioniel (L)
1957	THOMPSON, Sydney Herbert Stewart (SC)
1958	NUGMENT, Terence James (PC)
1962	NUGMENT, Terence James (PC)
1963	NUGMENT, Terence James (PC)
1965	NUGMENT, Terence James (PC)
1968	HARRIS, Hu (L)

Edmonton West
See: Edmonton

1917	GRIESBACH, William Antrobus (G)
1921	KENNEDY, Donald Macbeth (P)
1925	STEWART, Hon. Charles (L)
1926 *November 2, 1926	STEWART, Hon. Charles (L)
1930	STEWART, Hon. Charles (L)
1935	MacKINNON, James Angus (L)
1940	MacKINNON, Hon. James Angus (L)
1945	MacKINNON, Hon. James Angus (L)
1949	PRUDHAM, George (L)
1953	PRUDHAM, Hon. George (L)
1957	LAMBERT, Marcel (PC)
1958	LAMBERT, Marcel (PC)
1962	LAMBERT, Marcel (PC)
1963	LAMBERT, Marcel (PC)
1965	LAMBERT, Marcel (PC)
1968	LAMBERT, Marcel (PC)

Jasper-Edson
See: Peace River

1935	KUHL, Walter Frederick (SC)
1940	KUHL, Walter Frederick (ND)
1945	KUHL, Walter Frederick (SC)
1949	WELBOURN, John William (L)
1953	YUILL, Charles (SC)
1957	YUILL, Charles (SC)
1958	HORNER, Hugh Macarthur (PC)
1962	HORNER, Hugh Macarthur (PC)
1963	HORNER, Hugh Macarthur (PC)
1965	HORNER, Hugh Macarthur (PC)
1968 *November 6, 1967	HORNER, Hugh Macarthur (PC) CASTON, Douglas M. (PC)

See: Rocky Mountain House

Lethbridge
See: Medicine Hat

1917	BUCHANAN, William Ashbury (O)
1921	JELLIFF, Lincoln Henry (P)

1925	JELLIFF, Lincoln Henry (P)
1926	JELLIFF, Lincoln Henry (UFA)
1930	STEWART, John Smith (C)
1935	BLACKMORE, John Horne (SC)
1940	BLACKMORE, John Horne (ND)
1945	BLACKMORE, John Horne (SC)
1949	BLACKMORE, John Horne (SC)
1953	BLACKMORE, John Horne (SC)
1957	BLACKMORE, John Horne (SC)
1958	GUNDLOCK, Deane Roscoe (PC)
1962	GUNDLOCK, Deane Roscoe (PC)
1963	GUNDLOCK, Deane Roscoe (PC)
1965	GUNDLOCK, Deane Roscoe (PC)
1968	GUNDLOCK, Deane Roscoe (PC)

Macleod

1908	HERRON, John (C)
1911	WARNOCK, David (L)
1917	SHAW, Hugh Murray (G)
1921	COOTE, George Gibson (P)
1925	COOTE, George Gibson (P)
1926	COOTE, George Gibson (UFA)
1930	COOTE, George Gibson (UFA)
1935	HANSELL, Ernest George (SC)
1940	HANSELL, Ernest George (SC)
1945	HANSELL, Ernest George (SC)
1949	HANSELL, Ernest George (SC)
1953	HANSELL, Ernest George (SC)
1957	HANSELL, Ernest George (SC)
1958	KINDT, Lawrence Elliot (PC)
1962	KINDT, Lawrence Elliot (PC)
1963	KINDT, Lawrence Elliot (PC)
1965	KINDT, Lawrence Elliot (PC)

See: Crowfoot and Rocky Mountain House

Medicine Hat

1908	MAGRATH, Charles Alexander (C)
1911	BUCHANAN, William Ashbury (L)

1917	SIFTON, Hon. Arthur Lewis (G)
*June 27, 1921	
GARDINER, Robert (P)	
1921	GARDINER, Robert (P)
1925	GERSHAW, Frederick William (L)
1926	GERSHAW, Frederick William (L)
1930	GERSHAW, Frederick William (L)
1935	MITCHELL, Archibald Huge (SC)
1940	GERSHAW, Frederick William (L)
1945	WYLIE, William Duncan (SC)
1949	WYLIE, William Duncan (SC)
1953	WYLIE, William Duncan (SC)
1957	OLSON, Horace Andrew (SC)
1958	BURNSDEN, Edwin William (PC)
1962	OLSON, Horace Andrew (SC)
1963	OLSON, Horace Andrew (SC)
1965	OLSON, Horace Andrew (SC)
1968	OLSON, Horace Andrew (L)

Palliser (est. 1968)

| 1968 | SCHUMACHER, Stanley S. (PC) |

Peace River
See: Edmonton West

1925	KENNEDY, Donald Macbeth (P)
1926	KENNEDY, Donald Macbeth (UFA)
1930	KENNEDY, Donald Macbeth (UFA)
1935	PELLETIER, Rene-Antoine (SC)
1940	SISSONS, John Howard (L)
1945	LOW, Solon Earl (SC)
1949	LOW, Solon Earl (SC)
1953	LOW, Solon Earl (SC)
1957	LOW, Solon Earl (SC)
1958	BALDWIN, Gerald William (PC)
1962	BALDWIN, Gerald William (PC)
1963	BALDWIN, Gerald William (PC)
1965	BALDWIN, Gerald William (PC)

| 1968 | BALDWIN, Gerald William (PC) |

Red Deer
See: Calgary

1908	CLARK, Michael (L)
1911	CLARK, Michael (L)
1917	CLARK, Michael (G)
1921	SPEAKMAN, Alfred (P)
1925	SPEAKMAN, Alfred (P)
1926	SPEAKMAN, Alfred (UFA)
1930t	SPEAKMAN, Alfred (UFA)
1935	POOLE, Eric Joseph (SC)
1940	SHAW, Frederick Davis (ND)
1945	SHAW, Frederick Davis (SC)
1949	SHAW, Frederick Davis (SC)
1953	SHAW, Frederick Davis (SC)
1957	SHAW, Frederick Davis (SC)
1958	ROGERS, Harris (PC)
1962	THOMPSON, Robert Norman (SC)
1963	THOMPSON, Robert Norman (SC)
1965	THOMPSON, Robert Norman (SC)
1968	THOMPSON, Robert Norman (SC)

Strathcona

1904 * April 5, 1906	TALBOT, Peter (L) McINTYRE, Wilbert (L)
1908 *October 20, 1909	McINTYRE, Wilbert (L) DOUGLAS, James McCrie (L)
1911	DOUGLAS, James McCrie (L)
1917	DOUGLAS, James McCrie (G)
1921	Warner, Daniel Webster (P)

Vegreville
See: Victoria

1925	BOUTILLIER, Arthur Moren (P)
1926	LUCHKOVICH, Michael (UFA)
1930	LUCHKOVICH, Michael (UFA)
1935	HAYHURST, William (SC)
1940	HLYNKA, Anthony (ND)
1945	HLYNKA, Anthony (SC)
1949	DECORE, John (L)
1953	DECORE, John (L)
1957	STEFURA, Peter (SC)
1958	FANE, Frank John William (PC)
1962	FANE, Frank John William (PC)
1963	FANE, Frank John William (PC)
1965	FANE, Frank John William (PC)

| 1968 | MAZANKOWSKI, Donald Frank (PC) |

Victoria

1908	WHITE, William Henry (L)
1911	WHITE, William Henry (L)
1917	WHITE, William Henry (O)
1921	LUCAS, William Thomas (P)

Alphabetical List of Senators From Alberta 1905-1972

Analysis by religion and profession

Religion	Senator, Profession,
Roman Catholic	Ernest Aristide Blais
	Physician
Anglican	John A. "Buck" Buchanan
	Engineer
Methodist	William Ashbury Buchanan
	Publisher
Roman Catholic	Patrick Burns
	Rancher
United	Donald Cameron
	Educator
Roman Catholic	Jean Leon Cote
	Engineer
Anglican	Leverett George De Veber
	Physician
Roman Catholic	Amedée Forget
Lutheran	Frederick William Gershaw
	Physician

Anglican	James Gladstone
	Tribal chief/Farmer
Anglican	William Antrobus Griesbach
	Lawyer/Politician
Methodist	Richard Charles Hardisty
	Fur Trader
Methodist	William James Harmer
	Civil servant
United	Earl Adam Hastings
	Civil servant
Roman Catholic	Harry William Hays
	Rancher
Roman Catholic	Prosper Edmund Lessard
	Merchant
Anglican	Sir James A. Lougheed
	Lawyer
Presbyterian	James McKinnon
	Investment dealer
Baptist	Ernest Charles Manning
	Preacher
Methodist	Edward Michener
	Investment dealer
Anglican	J. Harper Prowse
	Lawyer/Politicians
Presbyterian	Daniel E. Riley
	Rancher
Methodist	George Henry Ross
	Lawyer

What's in a Name?

Roman Catholic	Philippe Roy
	Physician
United	J. Wesley Stambough
	Farmer
United	Peter Talbot
	Farmer/Politician

Maps and Charts

District of Alberta, Northwest Territories (1882-1905)

In 1870 the Canadian government acquired the former territories of the Hudson's Bay Company. Manitoba and "The Northwest Territories" officially became part of Canada on July 1870.

The Northwest Territories were initially governed by the Lieutenant-Governor of Manitoba; then by an 1880 Act of the Federal Government by their own Lieutenant-Governor and Council. Initially this Council was appointed, but after 1882 some councilors were elected. In 1888 a fully elective Assembly was created an in 1890 the Territorial Assembly was granted the powers of responsible government.

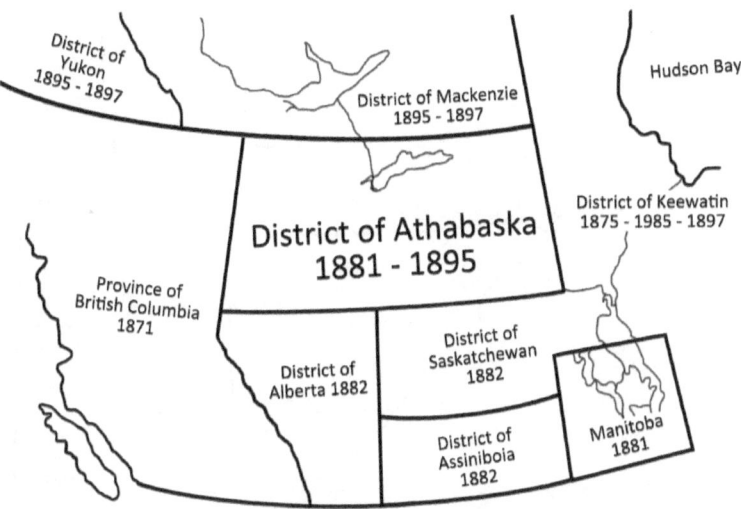

District of Athabasca: one of four provisional districts of the original Northwest Territories created in 1892 for federal administrative and postal purposes.

Northwest Territories 1904

Federal Ridings 1915

Federal Ridings 1934

What's in a Name?

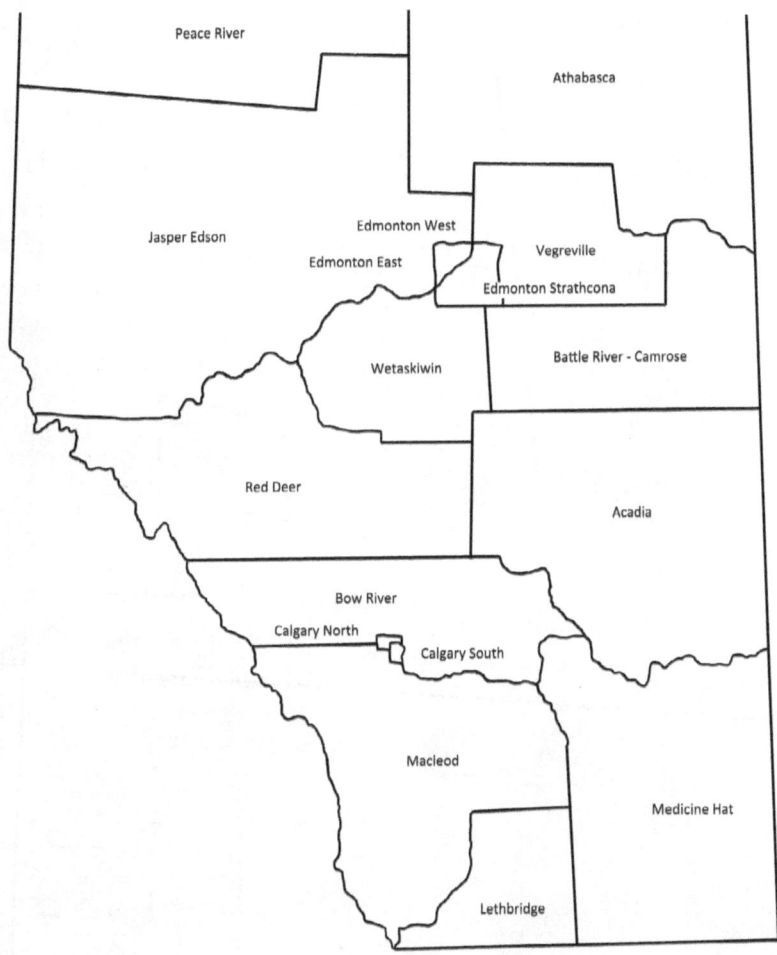

Federal Ridings Alberta 1952

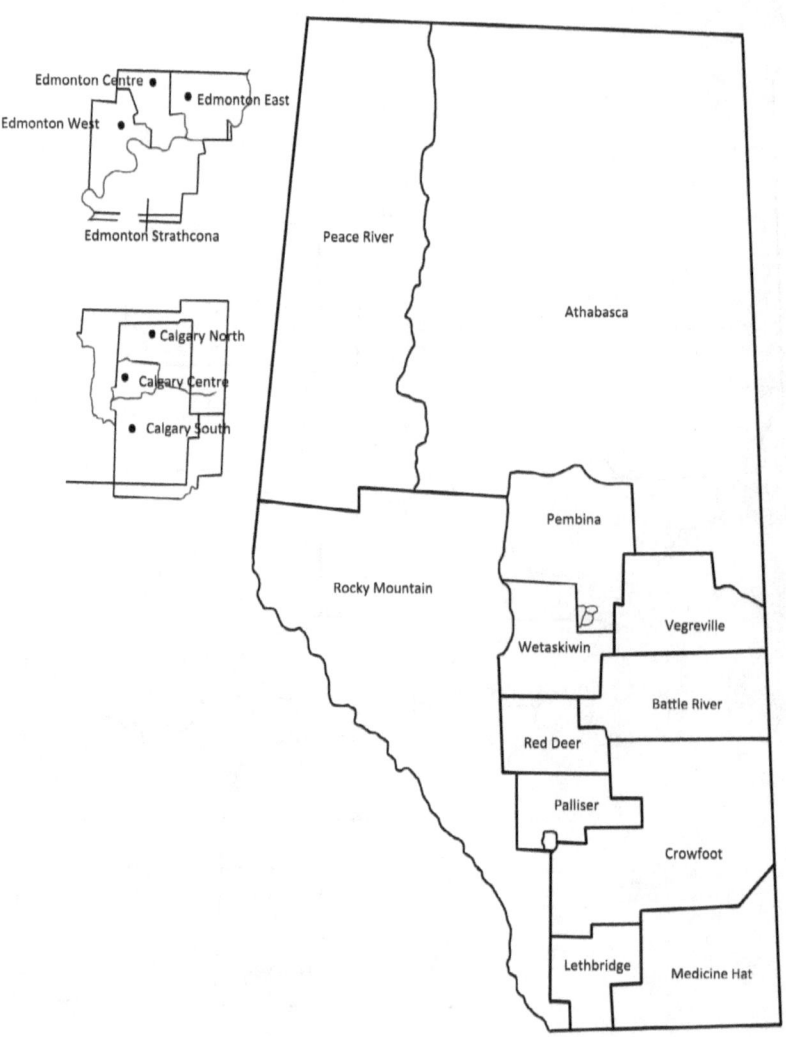

Federal Ridings 1972

Alberta Federal Representation

List of Alberta Federal Ridings

Alberta	1887 - 1908
Acadia	1925 - 1968
Athabasca	1925 - 1991
Battle River-Camrose	1953 - 1979
Beaver River	1988 - 1991
Bow River	1917 - 1967 & 1979 - 1991
Calgary	1904 - 1917
Calgary Centre	1968 - 1991
Calgary East	1917 – 1952 and 1979 – 1991
Calgary North	1953 – 1991
Calgary Northeast	1988 – 1991
Calgary South	1953 – 1991
Calgary Southeast	1988 – 1991
Calgary Southwest	1988 – 1991
Calgary West	1977 – 1952 & 1979 – 1991
Camrose	1925 – 1953
Crowfoot	1968 – 1991
Edmonton	1904 – 1917
Edmonton Centre	1968 – 1979
Edmonton East	1917 - 1991

ALBERTA
The Early Formative Years 1905-1921

Riding	1904	1908	1911	1917	1921
Battle River				Blair (Cons)	Spencer (UFA)
Bow River				Halladay (Union)	Garland (UFA)
Calgary East	McCarthy (Cons)		Bennett (Cons)	Redman (Union)	Irvine (Labour)
Calgary West				Tweedie (Cons)	Shaw (Labor)
Edmonton East	Oliver (Lib)			Mackie (Union)	Kellner (UFA)
Edmonton West				Griesbach (Cons)	Kennedy (UFA)
Lethbridge				Buchanan	Jelliff (UFA)
Macleod	Herron (Cons)		Warnock (Lib)	Shaw (Union)	Coote (UFA)
Medicine Hat		Magrath (Cons)	Buchanan (Lib)	Sifton (Union)	Gardiner (UFA)
Red Deer		Clark (Lib)			Speakman (UFA)
Strathcona	Talbot (Lib) /McIntyre (Lib)	McIntyre (Lib) / Douglas (Lib)			Warner (UFA)
Victoria		White (Lib)			Lucas (UFA)

United Farmers of Alberta Period 1921-1935

Riding	1921	1925	1926	1930	1935
Acadia		Gardiner (UFA)			Quelch (SC)
Athabasca		Cross (Lib)	Kellner (UFA)	Buckley (Lib)/Davies (Cons)	Rowe (SC)
Battle River	Spencer (UFA)				Fair (SC)
Camrose (Victoria)	Lucas (UFA)				Marshall (SC)
Bow River	Garland (UFA)				Johnston (SC)
Calgary East	Irvine (Labor)	Davis (Cons)	Adshead (Lib)	Stanley (Cons)	Landeryou (SC)
Calgary West	Shaw (UFA)	Bennett (Cons)	Blatchford (Lib)	Bury (Cons)	Hall (SC)
Edmonton East	Kellner (UFA)	Bury (Cons)	Blatchford (Lib)	Bury (Cons)	Hall (SC)
Edmonton West	Kennedy (UFA)	C. Stewart (Lib)			MacKinnon (Lib)
Jasper-Edson					
Lethbridge	Jelliff			J. Stewart	Blackmore (SC)
Macleod	Coote (UFA)				Hansell (SC)
Medicine Hat	Gardiner (UFA)	Gershaw (UFA)			Mitchell (SC)
Peace River		Kennedy (UFA)			Pelletier (SC)
Red Deer	Speakman (UFA)				Poole (SC)
Vegreville		Boutillier (UFA)	Luchkovich (UFA)		Hayhurst (SC)
Wetaskiwin (Strathcona)	Warner (UFA)	Tobin (Lib)	Irvine (UFA)		Jaques (SC)

What's in a Name?

The Social Credit Era in Alberta Federal Politics

Riding	1935	1940	1945	1949	1953	1957	1958
Acadia	Quelch (SC)						Horner (PC)
Athabasca	Rowe (SC)	Dechene (Lib)					Bigg (PC)
Battle River	Fair (SC)				Smith (SC)		Smallwood (PC)
Bow River	Johnston (SC)						
Camrose	Bennett (PC) / Cunnington (C)			Beyerstein (SC)			Wooliams (PC)
Calgary East (North)	Hall (SC) / Kennedy (SC)	Ross (Lib)	Harkness (PC)		Nickle		
Calgary West (South)		Edwards (Lib)	Smith (PC)				A. Smith (PC)
Edmonton East	Bennett (PC) / Cunnington (C)	F. / C. Casselman (L)	Ashby (SC)	Macdonald (L)	Holowach (SC)		Skoreyko (PC)

The Social Credit Era in Alberta Federal Politics (cont'd)

Riding	1935	1940	1945	1949	1953	1957	1958
Edmonton West	Hall (SC) / Kennedy (SC)			Prudham (Lib)		Lambert (PC)	
Edmonton Strathcona	MacKinnon (L)				Hanna (Lib)	Thompson (SC)	Nugent (PC)
Jasper-Edson	Kuhl (SC)			Welbourn (Lib)	Yuill (SC)		H. Horner (PC)
Lethbridge	Blackmore (SC)						Gundlock (PC)
Macleod	Hansell (SC)					Kindt (PC)	
Medicine Hat	Mitchell (SC)	Gershaw (Lib)	Wylie (SC)			Olson (SC)	Brunsden (PC)
Peace River	Pelletier (SC)	Sissons (Lib)	Low (SC)				Baldwin (PC)
Red Deer	Poole (SC)	Shaw (SC)					Rogers (PC)
Vegreville	Hayhurst (SC)	Hlynka (SC)		Decore (Lib)		Stefura (SC)	Fane (PC)
Wetaskiwin	Jaques (SC)			Thomas (SC)			Speakman (PC)

The Diefenbaker Years (1958-1972)

Riding	1958	1962	1963	1965	1968
Acadia	J. Horner (PC)				
Athabasca	Bigg (PC)				Yewchuk (PC)
Battle River	Smallwood (PC)				Downey (PC)
Bow River	Woolliams				Woolliams (PC)
Calgary North	Harkness (PC)				
Calgary South	A. Smith (PC)		Hays (Lib)	Ballard (PC)	Mahoney (Lib)
Calgary Centre					Harkness (PC)
Crowfoot					J. Horner (PC)
Edmonton Centre					Paproski (PC)
Edmonton East	Skoreyko (PC)				
Edmonton West	Lambert (PC)				
Edmonton-Strathcona	Nugent (PC)				Harris (Lib)
Jasper-Edson	H. Horner (PC)			Caston	
Lethbridge	Gundlock (PC)				

The Diefenbaker Years (1958-1972) (cont'd)

Riding	1958	1962	1963	1965	1968
Macleod	Kindt (PC)				
Medicine Hat	Brunsden (PC)	Olson (PC)			Olson (Lib)
Palliser					Schumacher (PC)
Peace River	Baldwin (PC)				
Pembina					Bigg (PC)
Red Deer	Rogers (PC)	Thompson (SC)			Thompson (PC)
Rocky Mountain House					Sulatycky (Lib)
Vegreville	Fane (PC)				Mazankowski (PC)
Wetaskiwin	Speakman (PC)	Moore (PC)			

Author

The Narrative Unity of the CURSOR MUNDI, 1970
Who's Who in Federal Politics from Alberta, 1972
Community Names of Alberta, 1972
The Conflict Between the Individual and Society in the Plays of James Bridie, 1973
Place Names of Southern Alberta, 1973
A Conspectus of the Contribution of HERODOTUS to the Development of Geographical Thought, 1990
International Law and Space Rescue Systems, 1991
Kensington Rune Stone and Other Essays, 1991

Translated (With Austin Mardon)

Munroe: A Description of the Western Isles of Scotland (1549)

Co-Authorship: Ernest Mardon and Austin Mardon

Alberta Mormon Politicians, 1991
The Alberta Judiciary Dictionary, 1990
Down and Out on an Ice Run in Moscow, 1992
Alberta Election Results 1882-1993, 1993
Edmonton Political Biographical Dictionary 1882-1990, 1997
Early Catholic Saints, 1997
Later Christian Saints, 1997
Childhood Memories and Legends of Christmas, 1998
Men of Dawn, 1999
United Farmers of Alberta, 1999
Alberta Catholic Politicians, 2001
Franco Albertan Politicians, 2001
Alberta Anglican Politicians, 2002
What's in a Name?, 2002

www.ingramcontent.com/pod-product-compliance
Lightning Source LLC
Chambersburg PA
CBHW031553300426
44111CB00006BA/298